Test Bank
to accompany

Introductory Statistics for the Behavioral Sciences
Fifth Edition

Joan Welkowitz
Robert B. Ewen
Jacob Cohen

Prepared by
Robert B. Ewen

Harcourt College Publishers

Fort Worth   Philadelphia   San Diego   New York   Orlando   Austin   San Antonio
Toronto   Montreal   London   Sydney   Tokyo

ISBN: 0-15-506910-1

Copyright © 2000 by Harcourt, Inc.

All rights reserved. No part of this publication may be reproduced or transmitted in any form or by any means, electronic or mechanical, including photocopy, recording, or any information storage and retrieval system, without permission in writing from the publisher, except that, until further notice, the contents or parts thereof may be reproduced for instructional purposes by users of INTRODUCTORY STATISTICS FOR THE BEHAVIORAL SCIENCES, Fifth Edition by Joan Welkowitz, Robert B. Ewen and Jacob Cohen.

Address for Domestic Orders
Harcourt College Publishers, 6277 Sea Harbor Drive, Orlando, FL 32887-6777
800-782-4479

Address for International Orders
International Customer Service
Harcourt, Inc., 6277 Sea Harbor Drive, Orlando, FL 32887-6777
407-345-3800
(fax) 407-345-4060
(e-mail) hbintl@harcourtbrace.com

Address for Editorial Correspondence
Harcourt College Publishers, 301 Commerce Street, Suite 3700, Fort Worth, TX 76102

Web Site Address
http://www.harcourtcollege.com

Printed in the United States of America

9 0 1 2 3 4 5 6 7 8   023   9 8 7 6 5 4 3 2 1

Harcourt College Publishers

Contents

Note to the Instructor   iv

Part I: Introduction
    1. Introduction   1

Part II: Descriptive Statistics
    2. Frequency Distributions and Graphs   11
    3. Transformed Scores I: Percentiles   19
    4. Measures of Central Tendency   27
    5. Measures of Variability   37
    6. Transformed Scores II: Z and T Scores   47
    7. Additional Techniques for Describing Batches of Data   57

Part III: Inferential Statistics
    8. The General Strategy of Inferential Statistics   65
    9. The Normal Curve Model   77
    10. Inferences About the Mean of a Single Population   87
    11. Testing Hypotheses About the Difference Between the Means of Two Populations   101
    12. Linear Correlation and Prediction   113
    13. Other Correlational Techniques   123
    14. Introduction to Power Analysis   129
    15. One-Way Analysis of Variance   135
    16. Introduction to Factorial Design: Two-Way Analysis of Variance   147
    17. Chi Square   157
    18. Nonparametric and Distribution-Free Methods   165

Note to the Instructor

To facilitate the use of different items on different tests (e.g., in different semesters, or for different classes during the same semester), a question may be asked in several different ways. Of course, it is not intended that such similar items be used on the same examination.

Some questions use the following format:

Florida is located in:
  (a) The United States
  (b) North America
* (c) *Both* of the above
  (d) *Neither* of the above

When "both of the above" is the correct answer, giving half credit for answers (a) and (b) will reward students for knowing part of the answer while giving the most credit to students who select the best answer. Instructors who prefer not to use this format can readily convert such questions to true-false questions:

1. Florida is located in the United States.
   * (a) True
     (b) False

2. Florida is located in North America.
   * (a) True
     (b) False

Chapter 1

1. The purpose of *descriptive statistics* is to: (p. 5)
    (a) draw conclusions about a group that is too large to measure.
    * (b) summarize important characteristics of a set of data.
    (c) *both* of the above
    (d) *neither* of the above

2. The purpose of inferential statistics is to: (p. 5)
    * (a) draw conclusions about a group that is too large to measure.
    (b) summarize important characteristics of a set of data.
    (c) draw inferences about the sample that the researcher is studying.
    (d) *none* of the above

3. You need a convenient way to tell a friend about all of the grades (p. 5)
   you have received in college, so you say that your grade-point average is 3.27.
   This is an example of a(n)
    * (a) descriptive statistic.
    (b) inferential statistic.
    (c) parameter.
    (d) population.

4. Why are *inferential statistics* used in the behavioral sciences? (p. 5)
    (a) To correct for the error in tests, questionnaires, and other research instruments.
    (b) A science must use numerical values.
    (c) Researchers need a way to summarize the large amounts of data that they obtain.
    * (d) Researchers want to draw conclusions about groups that are too large to measure in their entirety.

5. As used in statistics, the term *population* refers to: (p. 5)
    (a) only human beings, such as all American citizens.
    (b) all of the numerical data collected by the researcher.
    * (c) a large group of people, animals, or responses that are alike in at least one respect.
    (d) the group of people studied by the researcher.

6. As used in statistics, the term *sample* refers to: (p. 5)
   * (a) a relatively small number of people drawn from a specified population.
   (b) all of the cases about which the researcher wishes to draw conclusions.
   (c) the tests, questionnaires, and other instruments used by the researcher.
   (d) the minimum number of people that a research study should include.

7. Researchers in the behavioral sciences wish to draw conclusions about: (p. 5)
   (a) descriptive statistics.
   (b) inferential statistics.
   * (c) one or more populations.
   (d) one or more samples.

8. The numerical values computed by the researcher, based on the data obtained from the research study, are called *parameters*. (p. 6)
   (a) True
   * (b) False

9. As used in statistics, the term *generalize* refers to: (p. 6)
   (a) how carefully the sample was drawn.
   (b) the probability that the research results are incorrect.
   (c) the probability that the research results are correct.
   * (d) the group to whom the research results should be applied.

10. A researcher uses a sample of 100 African-American women. This sample is: (p. 6)
    (a) incorrectly drawn because no whites or males are included.
    (b) too small to provide any useful results.
    (c) too large and inconvenient to study.
    * (d) correctly drawn if the researcher wishes to draw conclusions only about African-American women.

Questions 11–28 refer to the small group of data shown below.

X data: $X_1 = 4$ $X_2 = 2$ $X_3 = 0$ $X_4 = 4$
Y data: $Y_1 = 3$ $Y_2 = 1$ $Y_3 = 1$

11. ΣX is equal to: (p. 7)
    (a) 3
    (b) 4
    (c) 5
    * (d) 10

12. ΣY is equal to: (p. 7)
    (a) 3
    (b) 4
    * (c) 5
    (d) 10

13. N_X is equal to: (p. 7)
    (a) 3
    * b) 4
    (c) 5
    (d) 10

14. N_Y is equal to: (p. 7)
    * (a) 3
    (b) 4
    (c) 5
    (d) 10

15. $(\Sigma X)(\Sigma Y)$ is equal to: (p. 9)
    (a) 0
    (b) 14
    (c) 15
    * (d) 50

16. $\Sigma X + \Sigma Y$ is equal to: (p. 8)
    (a) 5
    (b) 10
    (c) 11
    * (d) 15

17. $\Sigma X - \Sigma Y$ is equal to: (p. 9)
    (a) 1
    * (b) 5
    (c) 10
    (d) 15

18. $\sum Y - \sum X$ is equal to: (p. 9)
    * (a) −5
    (b) 0
    (c) 5
    (d) 10

19. $(\sum X)^2$ is equal to: (p. 10)
    (a) 11
    (b) 25
    (c) 36
    * (d) 100

20. $\sum X^2$ is equal to: (p. 10)
    (a) 11
    (b) 25
    * (c) 36
    (d) 100

21. $(\sum Y)^2$ is equal to: (p. 10)
    (a) 11
    * (b) 25
    (c) 36
    (d) 100

22. $\sum Y^2$ is equal to: (p. 10)
    * (a) 11
    (b) 25
    (c) 36
    (d) 100

23. If $k = 2$, $\sum (X + k)$ is equal to: (p. 11)
    (a) 12
    (b) 16
    * (c) 18
    (d) 20

24. If $k = 2$, $\sum (X - k)$ is equal to: (p. 11)
    (a) 0
    * (b) 2
    (c) 4
    (d) 8

25. If k = 3, $\Sigma(Y + k)$ is equal to: (p. 11)
    (a) 8
    (b) 11
    * (c) 14
    (d) 17

26. If k = 3, $\Sigma(Y - k)$ is equal to: (p. 11)
    * (a) −4
    (b) 0
    (c) 1
    (d) 2

27. If k = 2, ΣkX is equal to: (p. 11)
    (a) 10
    (b) 12
    (c) 18
    * (d) 20

28. If k = 3, ΣkY is equal to: (p. 11)
    (a) 8
    (b) 14
    * (c) 15
    (d) 30

Questions 29–45 refer to the small group of data shown below.

S	X	V
1	2	0
2	1	4
3	2	3

29. ΣX is equal to: (p. 7)
    (a) 3
    * (b) 5
    (c) 7
    (d) 12

30. ΣY is equal to: (p. 7)
    (a) 3
    (b) 5
    * (c) 7
    (d) 12

31. $(\Sigma X)(\Sigma Y)$ is equal to: (p. 9)
    (a) 0
    (b) 10
    (c) 12
    * (d) 35

32. ΣXY is equal to: (p. 9)
    (a) 0
    * (b) 10
    (c) 12
    (d) 35

33. $\Sigma X + \Sigma Y$ is equal to: (p. 8)
    (a) 5
    (b) 7
    (c) 10
    * (d) 12

34. $\Sigma X - \Sigma Y$ is equal to: (p. 9)
    (a) −4
    * (b) −2
    (c) 2
    (d) 4

35. $\Sigma Y - \Sigma X$ is equal to: (p. 9)
    (a) −4
    (b) −2
    * (c) 2
    (d) 4

36. $(\Sigma X)^2$ is equal to: (p. 10)
    (a) 9
    (b) 16
    * (c) 25
    (d) 49

37. ΣX^2 is equal to: (p. 10)
    * (a) 9
    (b) 16
    (c) 25
    (d) 49

38. $(\Sigma Y)^2$ is equal to: (p. 10)
    (a) 9
    (b) 16
    (c) 25
    * (d) 49

39. ΣY^2 is equal to: (p. 10)
    (a) 9
    (b) 16
    * (c) 25
    (d) 49

40. If $k = 5$, $\Sigma(X + k)$ is equal to: (p. 11)
    (a) 10
    (b) 15
    * (c) 20
    (d) 25

41. If $k = 5$, $\Sigma(X - k)$ is equal to: (p. 11)
    * (a) −10
    (b) −5
    (c) 0
    (d) 5

42. If k = 10, $\Sigma(Y + k)$ is equal to: (p. 11)
    (a) 17
    (b) 27
    * (c) 37
    (d) 47

43. If k = 10, $\Sigma(Y - k)$ is equal to: (p. 11)
    (a) −30
    * (b) −23
    (c) −13
    (d) −3

44. If k = 5, ΣkX is equal to: (p. 11)
    (a) 10
    (b) 15
    (c) 20
    * (d) 25

45. If k = 10, ΣkY is equal to: (p. 11)
    (a) 0
    (b) 17
    (c) 37
    * (d) 70

Questions 46–57 refer to the small group of data shown below.

S	A	B	C
1	1	2	2
2	0	3	1
3	4	0	6
4	2	5	1
5	1	2	3

46. ΣAB is equal to: (p. 9)
    (a) 13
    * (b) 14
    (c) 20
    (d) 96

47. $\Sum AC$ is equal to: (p. 9)
    (a) 20
    (b) 21
    * (c) 31
    (d) 104

48. $\Sum BC$ is equal to: (p. 9)
    * (a) 18
    (b) 25
    (c) 31
    (d) 156

49. $(\Sum A)(\Sum B)$ is equal to: (p. 9)
    (a) 13
    (b) 14
    (c) 20
    * (d) 96

50. $(\Sum A)(\Sum C)$ is equal to: (p. 9)
    (a) 20
    (b) 21
    (c) 31
    * (d) 104

51. $(\Sum B)(\Sum C)$ is equal to: (p. 9)
    (a) 18
    (b) 25
    (c) 31
    * (d) 156

52. $\Sum A^2$ is equal to: (p. 10)
    (a) 8
    * (b) 22
    (c) 25
    (d) 64

53. $(\Sigma A)^2$ is equal to: (p. 10)
    (a) 8
    (b) 22
    (c) 25
    * (d) 64

54. ΣB^2 is equal to: (p. 10)
    (a) 12
    (b) 15
    * (c) 42
    (d) 144

55. $(\Sigma B)^2$ is equal to: (p. 10)
    (a) 12
    (b) 15
    (c) 42
    * (d) 144

56. ΣC^2 is equal to: (p. 10)
    (a) 13
    (b) 36
    * (c) 51
    (d) 169

57. $(\Sigma C)^2$ is equal to: (p. 10)
    (a) 13
    (b) 36
    (c) 51
    * (d) 169

Chapter 2

1. The purpose of *frequency distributions* is: (p. 18)
   * (a) only descriptive—to conveniently summarize and describe large quantities of data.
   (b) only inferential—to draw conclusions about a group that is too large to measure.
   (c) either descriptive or inferential, depending on the goals of the researcher.
   (d) neither descriptive nor inferential.

2. If 100 students take a 10-point quiz, one correct way to summarize this information is to use: (pp. 18–23)
   (a) a grouped frequency distribution.
   * (b) a regular frequency distribution.
   (c) either a regular or grouped frequency distribution, depending on the goals of the researcher.
   (d) neither a regular nor a grouped frequency distribution.

3. One serious problem with *grouped* frequency distributions is that they: (p. 23)
   (a) require a great deal of time and effort.
   (b) do not look as neat and concise as regular frequency distributions.
   (c) are not suitable for very large samples.
   * (d) lose information.

4. A frequency distribution must always begin with zero. (p. 23)
   (a) True
   * (b) False

5. An interval size of 4 is usually *not* used for grouped frequency distributions. (p. 23)
   * (a) True
   (b) False

6. When constructing a grouped frequency distribution, the total number of intervals should be approximately: (p. 23)
   (a) 2 to 5.
   (b) 5 to 10.
   * (c) 8 to 15.
   (d) 5 to 25.

7. If you're using an interval size of 3, which of the following is not an acceptable value for the *lowest score* in an interval? (p. 23)
   (a) 0
   (b) 3
   * (c) 10
   (d) 99

8. If you're using an interval size of 5, which of the following is *not* an acceptable value for the *lowest score* in an interval? (p. 23)
   (a) 0
   * (b) 1
   (c) 5
   (d) 100

9. A *histogram* displays data by using: (p. 24)
   * (a) bars.
   (b) cumulative frequencies.
   (c) points on a graph that are connected.
   (d) "stems" and "leaves."

10. A *histogram* would be best for displaying: (p. 25)
    (a) scores on an IQ test.
    (b) family income.
    (c) results of a 100-point midterm exam.
    * (d) number of children per family.

11. A *regular frequency distribution* displays data by using: (p. 26)
    (a) bars.
    (b) cumulative frequencies.
    * (c) points on a graph that are connected.
    (d) "stems" and "leaves."

12. A *regular frequency distribution* would be best for displaying ALL of the following EXCEPT: (p. 27)
    (a) scores on a measure of introversion-extraversion.
    * (b) how many dreams people have during one night.
    (c) speed of rats running a T-maze to get a food reward.
    (d) results of a 10-point psychology quiz.

13. A frequency distribution is *symmetric* if it: (p. 28)
    (a) has only one peak.
    (b) has at least two peaks.
    * (c) can be divided into two mirror-image halves.
    (d) has a long "tail" at one end.

14. A frequency distribution is *unimodal* if it: (p. 29)
    * (a) has only one peak.
    (b) has at least two peaks.
    (c) can be divided into two mirror-image halves.
    (d) Has a long "tail" at one end.

15. A frequency distribution is *skewed* if: (p. 28)
    (a) has only one peak.
    (b) has at least two peaks.
    (c) can be divided into two mirror-image halves.
    * (d) has a long "tail" at one end.

16. Which of the following describes a *J-curve*? (p. 29)
    (a) Everyone receives exactly the same score.
    (b) The distribution has two peaks, one slightly larger than the other.
    * (c) Most people score zero, some people score one, a few people score two, and very few people score higher than two.
    (d) Most people score at the center of the distribution, and as you go farther from the center, there are fewer scores.

17. A distribution that is *skewed to the right* would have: (p. 28)
    (a) a small number of very low scores.
    * (b) a small number of very high scores.
    (c) *both* of the above
    (d) *neither* of the above

18. A very difficult exam would be likely to produce a distribution that is: (p. 28)
    (a) negatively skewed.
    * (b) positively skewed.
    (c) unimodal and symmetric.
    (d) rectangular.

19. A very easy exam would be likely to produce a distribution that is: (p. 28)
    * (a) negatively skewed.
    (b) positively skewed.
    (c) unimodal and symmetric.
    (d) rectangular.

Harcourt, Inc.

20. Scores on a standardized intelligence test are likely to produce a distribution that is: (p. 29)
    (a) skewed to the left.
    (b) skewed to the right.
    * (c) unimodal and symmetric.
    (d) a J-curve.

21. The number of accidents at work during one month is likely to produce a distribution that is: (p. 29)
    (a) skewed to the left.
    (b) rectangular.
    (c) unimodal and symmetric.
    * (d) a J-curve.

22. If a roulette wheel is fair, the number of times each number pays off would produce a distribution that is: (p. 29)
    (a) skewed to the left.
    * (b) rectangular.
    (c) unimodal and symmetric.
    (d) a J-curve.

23. In a frequency distribution, the letter *f* denotes: (p. 19)
    * (a) the number of times each score occurs.
    (b) the possible score values.
    (c) how many scores were lower than a given score.
    (d) the interval size.

24. For which of the following sets of scores should a *grouped* frequency distribution be used? (p. 23)
    (a) Set A: 87, 100, 98, 90, 92, 94, 94, 95, 88, 91, 99, 92, 89
    (b) Set B: 7, 4, 6, 9, 10, 2, 0, 10, 8, 7, 7, 4, 5, 6, 6, 5, 8
    (c) Set C: 35.8, 34.2, 40.1, 31.6, 41.7, 32.8, 29.5
    * (d) *None* of the above

25. For which of the following sets of scores should a *grouped* frequency distribution be used? (p. 23)
    (a) Set A: 79, 72, 81, 77, 84, 80, 83, 78, 77, 81
    (b) Set B: 1083, 1279, 406
    * (c) Set C: 97, 46, 82, 65, 77, 89, 67, 58, 92, 87, 75, 74, 73, 81, 87, 82, 75, 76, 84, 87, 92, 54, 62, 51, 88, 75, 73, 78, 80
    (d) Set D: 7, 10, 8, 5, 6, 12, 0, 4, 11, 7, 3, 5, 8, 6, 7, 2, 9, 8, 11, 10, 1, 11, 12, 7, 5, 3, 4, 6, 11, 10, 8, 7, 6, 5, 5, 3

Questions 26–30 refer to the set of data shown below:

X	f	cf
10	1	19
9	2	18
7	7	16
6	3	9
5	4	6
3	1	2
2	1	1

No one obtained scores of 0, 1, 4, or 8.

26. What mistake was made in constructing this frequency distribution? (p. 19)
    (a) not beginning at zero
    * (b) omitting the score values 4 and 8 from the frequency distribution
    (c) not using a grouped frequency distribution
    (d) having cf and f in the same table

27. How many people (scores) are there? (pp. 19, 21)
    * (a) 19
    (b) 42
    (c) 66
    (d) There is no way to tell from the information given.

28. How many people obtained scores of *7 or less*? (pp. 20–21)
    (a) 7
    (b) 9
    * (c) 16
    (d) 18

29. How many modes does this distribution have? (p. 29)
    (a) 0
    * (b) 1
    (c) 2
    (d) More than 2

30. Is this distribution symmetric? (p. 28)
    * (a) No
    (b) Yes

Questions 31–35 refer to the set of data shown below:

X	f	cf
13–14	1	17
11–12	4	16
9–10	7	12
7–8	4	5
5–6	1	1

31. What mistake(s) was/were made in constructing this frequency distribution?   (p. 19)
    (a) Intervals do not begin with an even multiple of the interval size.
    (b) A regular frequency distribution should have been used.
    (c) There are too few intervals.
    * (d) *All* of the above
    (e) *None* of the above

32. How many people (scores) are there?   (pp. 19, 21)
    (a) 5
    * (b) 17
    (c) 51
    (d) There is no way to tell from the information given.

33. How many people obtained scores of *10 or less*?   (pp. 20–31)
    (a) 5
    (b) 7
    * (c) 12
    (d) 16

34. How many modes does this distribution have?   (p. 29)
    (a) 0
    * (b) 1
    (c) 2
    (d) More than 2

35. Is this distribution symmetric?   (p. 28)
    (a) No
    * (b) Yes

Questions 36–40 refer to the set of data shown below:

X	f	cf
47	1	28
46	2	27
45	6	25
44	3	19
43	1	16
42	2	15
41	7	13
40	2	6
39	3	4
38	1	1

36. What mistake was made in constructing this frequency distribution? (pp. 19, 23)
    - (a) A grouped frequency distribution should have been used.
    - (b) There are too few intervals.
    - (c) Not beginning at zero
    - * (d) *None* of the above

37. How many people (scores) are there? (pp. 19, 21)
    - (a) 10
    - * (b) 28
    - (c) 154
    - (d) There is no way to tell from the information given.

38. How many people obtained scores of *43 or less*? (pp. 20–21)
    - (a) 1
    - (b) 15
    - * (c) 16
    - (d) 19

39. How many modes does this distribution have? (p. 29)
    - (a) 0
    - (b) 1
    - * (c) 2
    - (d) More than 2

40. How many people obtained scores of *41 or more*? (p. 21)
    - (a) 6
    - (b) 7
    - * (c) 22
    - (d) 24

Chapter 3

1. Why is it useful to convert a raw score to a percentile rank? (p. 33)
    - (a) We can draw inferences about a population that is too large to measure.
    - (b) We can summarize a group of scores more concisely.
    - *(c) to show how the raw score compares to the scores of a specific group
    - (d) to show the percent of total points that was obtained

2. A percentile rank of 10 means that the score is in the top 10 percent of the group—90 percent of the scores were lower. (p. 33)
    - (a) True
    - *(b) False

3. A student obtains a score of 76 on a 100-point midterm exam. The score of 76 is called a: (p. 33)
    - (a) percentile.
    - (b) percentile rank.
    - *(c) raw score.
    - (d) transformed score.

4. Which of the following is a *raw score*? (p. 33)
    - (a) An SAT score of 530
    - (b) A percentile rank of 82
    - (c) A Z score of +1.10
    - *(d) A score of 7 on a 10-point quiz

5. The *score* at or below which a given percent of the cases fall is called a: (p. 33)
    - *(a) percentile.
    - (b) percentile rank.
    - (c) transformed score.
    - (d) Z score.

6. The *percent of cases* in a specific reference group scoring at or below a given score is called a: (p. 33)
    - (a) percentile.
    - *(b) percentile rank.
    - (c) transformed score.
    - (d) Z score.

7. Mary's score on Test X has a percentile rank of 85. John's score on Test Y (p. 33) has a percentile rank of 81. Can we conclude that Mary did better than John?
   (a) Yes, because 85 is larger than 81.
   (b) No, because 85 and 81 are only 4 points apart.
   * (c) No, because John's test might have been more difficult than Mary's test.
   (d) No, because we don't know how many total points there were on each test.

8. Which of the following represents the best performance? (p. 34)
   * (a) A percentile rank of 72 on the Graduate Record Examination (given to college graduates)
   (b) A percentile rank of 72 on the Scholastic Aptitude Test (given to high-school graduates)
   (c) A percentile rank of 72 on a test of general ability given to all American adults
   (d) *None* of the above—performance is equal since the percentile ranks are the same

9. In a grouped frequency distribution, the *lower real limit* of the 24–26 (p. 35) interval is 24.0.
   (a) True
   * (b) False

10. In a regular frequency distribution, the lower real limit of the score (pp. 35–36) of 4 is 3.5.
    * (a) True
    (b) False

11. A *percentile* divides the total number of cases into how many equal parts? (p. 41)
    (a) 2
    (b) 4
    (c) 10
    * (d) 100

12. A *quartile* divides the total number of cases into how many equal parts? (p. 41)
    (a) 2
    * (b) 4
    (c) 10
    (d) 100

13. A *decile* divides the total number of cases into how many equal parts? (p. 41)
    (a) 2
    (b) 4
    * (c) 10
    (d) 100

14. The *median* divides the total number of cases into how many equal parts? (p. 41)
    * (a) 2
    (b) 4
    (c) 10
    (d) 100

15. The *median* is equal to: (p. 41)
    (a) the second quartile.
    (b) the fifth decile.
    (c) the 50th percentile.
    * (d) *all* of the above
    (e) *none* of the above

16. Which of the following represents the best performance? (p. 41)
    * (a) The second quartile
    (b) The third decile
    (c) The 25th percentile
    (d) The 10th percentile

17. Which of the following represents the best performance? (p. 41)
    (a) The 40th percentile
    (b) The first decile
    (c) The median
    * (c) The third quartile

18. Which of the following represents the best performance? (p. 41)
    (a) The first quartile
    (b) The fourth decile
    * (c) The median
    (d) The 30th percentile

19. Which of the following represents the best performance? (p. 41)
    (a) The third quartile
    * (b) The 80th percentile
    (c) The median
    (d) The sixth decile

20. Which of the following represents the best performance? (p. 41)
    (a) The second quartile
    (b) The 60th percentile
    (c) The median
    * (d) The seventh decile

21. Twenty students take a 10-point quiz, and John obtains a score of 7. (pp. 34–37)
    Eight students scored lower than 7. Given only this information, which of
    the following must be true?
    * (a) John's percentile rank cannot be lower than 42.5.
    (b) John's percentile rank must be less than 50.
    (c) John cannot have received the highest score.
    (d) John's percentile rank must be higher than 50.

22. Ten students take a 10-point quiz, and Mary obtains a score of 6. (pp. 34–37)
    Three students scored lower than 6. Given only this information, which of
    the following must be true?
    (a) Mary must be below average.
    (b) Mary cannot have received the highest score.
    * (c) Mary could have a percentile rank as high as 65.
    (d) Mary cannot have a percentile rank higher than 30.

23. Ten students take a 10-point quiz, and Sam obtains a score of 8. (pp. 34–37)
    Seven students scored below 8, one scored 9, and one scored 10.
    Given only this information, which of the following must be true?
    (a) Sam's percentile rank is 70.
    * (b) Sam's percentile rank is 75.
    (c) Sam's percentile rank must be less than 50.
    (d) Sam's percentile rank must be higher than 80.

24. Fifty students take a 100-point midterm exam, and Ellen scores 72. (pp. 34–37)
    If three other students also scored 72, 10 students scored below 72,
    and everyone else scored higher than 72, what is Ellen's percentile rank?
    (a) 20
    (b) 22
    * (c) 24
    (d) Cannot be computed from the information given

25. Fifty students take a 100-point midterm exam, and James scores 90. (pp. 34–37)
    If 44 students obtained scores below 90 and five obtained scores higher
    than 90, what is James's percentile rank?
    (a) 88
    * (b) 89
    (c) 90
    (d) Cannot be computed from the information given

26. Fifty students take a 100-point midterm exam, and Tricia scores 86. (pp. 34–37)
    If 40 students obtained scores below 86, what is Tricia's percentile rank?
    (a) 80
    (b) 81
    * (c) Cannot be determined from the information given but must be at least 81
    (d) Cannot be determined from the information given but cannot be higher than 80

27. One hundred students take a 50-point test, and Richard scores 34. (pp. 34–37)
    If 20 students score higher than 34, one other student scores 34,
    and everyone else scores below 34, what is Richard's percentile rank?
    (a) 20
    (b) 21
    * (c) 79
    (d) Cannot be determined from the information given

28. One hundred students take a 50-point test, and Joanne scores 40. (pp. 34–37)
    If 11 other students also score 40, 68 students score below 40, and
    the rest score above 40, what is Joanne's percentile rank?
    (a) 68
    * (b) 74
    (c) 80
    (d) Cannot be determined from the information given

29. One hundred students take a 50-point test, and Mary's score of 49 (pp. 34–37)
    is the highest in the class. No one else scored 49 or 50. What is Mary's
    percentile rank?
    (a) 99
    * (b) 99.5
    (c) 100
    (d) Cannot be determined from the information given

30. One hundred students take a 50-point test, and William's score of 8 (pp. 34–37)
    is the lowest in the class. No one else scored 8 or less. What is William's
    percentile rank?
    (a) 0
    * (b) 0.5
    (c) 1
    (d) Cannot be determined from the information given

31. Twenty students take a 10-point quiz. If all of the students obtain (pp. 34–37)
exactly the same score, what is each student's percentile rank?
    (a) 0
    (b) 49.5
    * (c) 50
    (d) Cannot be determined from the information given

32. Twenty students take a 10-point quiz. If nine students score 5 or less, (p. 41)
and the other 11 students score higher than 5, the median must be:
    (a) less than 6.
    (b) 6.0.
    (c) between 5.5 and 6.5.
    * (d) between 5.5 and 9.6.

Questions 33–35 refer to the data shown below:

X	f	cf
10	1	20
9	0	19
8	2	19
7	5	17
6	4	12
5	2	8
4	3	6
3	2	3
2	0	1
1	0	1
0	1	1

33. The score that corresponds to the 70th percentile is approximately: (pp. 37–39)
    (a) 8
    * (b) 7
    (c) 6
    (d) 3

34. The score that corresponds to the 50th percentile is approximately: (pp. 37–39)
    (a) 8
    (b) 7
    * (c) 6
    (d) 3

35. The *percentile rank* corresponding to a score of 9: (pp. 34–37)
    (a) cannot be computed because no one obtained a score of 9.
    (b) is the same as for a score of 8.
    (c) is equal to 90.
    * (d) is equal to 95.

Questions 36–42 refer to the set of data shown below:

X	f	cf
27–29	1	20
24–26	3	19
21–23	4	16
18–20	5	12
15–17	2	7
12–14	1	5
9–11	2	4
6–8	1	2
3–5	0	1
0–2	1	1

36. The score corresponding to the 90th percentile is approximately: (pp. 34–37)
    (a) 21
    (b) 22
    (c) 23
    * (d) 24

37. The median is approximately: (p. 41)
    (a) 16
    (b) 17
    * (c) 19
    (d) 22

38. For this set of data, a score of 3 and a score of 4 have the same percentile rank. (pp. 34–37)
    * (a) True
    (b) False

39. A percentile rank for scores of 3, 4, and 5 cannot be computed for this set of data because no one obtained these scores. (pp. 34–37)
    (a) True
    * (b) False

40. A score of 9 has a percentile rank of approximately: (pp. 34–37)
    (a) 5
    (b) 10
    * (c) 12
    (d) 20

41. A score of 23 has a percentile rank of approximately: (pp. 34–37)
    (a) 60
    (b) 63
    (c) 70
    * (d) 77

42. For this set of data, a score of 27 and a score of 28 have the same (pp. 34–37)
    percentile rank.
    (a) True
    * (b) False

Chapter 4

1. The mean and the median are measures of: (p. 44)
   * (a) the general location of a set of scores.
   (b) how spread out the scores in a set of data are from one another.
   (c) *both* of the above
   (d) *neither* of the above

2. Two classes take a 10-point quiz, and the results are: (p. 45)
   Class A: 9, 8, 8, 7, 4, 4, 3, 2, 0
   Class B: 7, 7, 6, 5, 5, 5, 4, 3, 3
   The mean for each class is 5.0. A score of 7 is:
   (a) better in class A.
   * (b) better in class B.
   (c) just as good in both classes because the means are the same.

3. Two classes take a 10-point quiz, and the results are: (p. 45)
   Class A: 9, 8, 8, 7, 4, 4, 3, 2, 0
   Class B: 7, 7, 6, 5, 5, 5, 4, 3, 3
   The mean for each class is 5.0. A score of 3 is:
   * (a) better in class A.
   (b) better in class B.
   (c) just as good in both classes because the means are the same.

4. If $\Sigma X = 60$ and $N = 20$, $\overline{X}$ is equal to: (p. 46)
   (a) 0.33
   * (b) 3.0
   (c) 33.0
   (d) Cannot be determined from the information given

5. If $\Sigma Y = 22$ and $N = 5$, $\overline{Y}$ is equal to: (p. 46)
   (a) 0.2
   * (b) 4.5
   (c) 22.0
   (d) Cannot be determined from the information given

6. The sum of the distances (deviations) of all scores from the mean is: (p. 46)
    * (a) always equal to zero.
    (b) always equal to 1.0.
    (c) always equal to N.
    (d) different for different groups of data.

7. A class takes a 10-point quiz, and the results are: (p. 48)
    Class X: 9, 8, 8, 7, 4, 4, 3, 2, 0
    If the score of 9 is changed to 45, what will happen to the mean?
    (a) It will remain the same.
    (b) It will increase by less than 1 point.
    * (c) It will increase by 4 points.
    (d) Cannot be determined from the information given

8. A class takes a 100-point midterm, and the results are: (p. 48)
    Class Y: 99, 97, 97, 94, 93, 90, 90, 88, 85, 81
    If the score of 81 is changed to 31, what will happen to the mean?
    (a) It will remain the same.
    (b) It will decrease by less than 1 point.
    * (c) It will decrease by 5 points.
    (d) Cannot be determined from the information given

9. ALL of the following are *advantages* of using the *mean* EXCEPT: (p. 48)
    (a) it takes all of the scores into account.
    (b) it is the most consistent measure of central tendency across different samples drawn from the same population.
    (c) it can be used in many kinds of statistical analyses.
    * (d) it is *not* affected by extreme scores at the high or low end of the distribution.

10. The *median* is the best measure of central tendency to use when: (p. 49)
    (a) you plan to use this measure in many statistical analyses.
    (b) you want to take all of the scores into account.
    (c) the sample size is very large.
    * (d) the exact size of the largest scores is unknown.

Questions 11–22 refer to the data shown below.

X	f	cf
10	2	20
9	0	18
8	1	18
7	5	17
6	4	12
5	4	8
4	1	4
3	3	3
2	0	0
1	0	0
0	0	0

11. The median divides this set of scores so that: (p. 49)
    (a) five scores fall below the median and five scores fall above it.
  * (b) 10 scores fall below the median and 10 scores fall above it.
    (c) eight scores fall below the median and 12 scores fall above it.
    (d) *none* of the above

12. The median of this set of scores is equal to: (p. 49)
    (a) 5.0
    (b) 5.5
  * (c) 6.0
    (d) 6.5

13. The *mean* of this set of scores is equal to: (p. 47)
    (a) 2.0
    (b) 2.75
  * (c) 6.0
    (d) Cannot be determined from the information given

14. A comparison of the mean and median indicates that this set of data is: (p. 50)
    (a) rectangular.
    (b) negatively skewed.
    (c) positively skewed.
  * (d) *none* of the above

Harcourt, Inc.

15. If one score of 8 is changed to 10, which of the following will change? (p. 50)
    * (a) Only the mean
    (b) Only the median
    (c) *Both* the mean and the median
    (d) *Neither* the mean nor the median

16. If one score of 3 is changed to 9, which of the following will change? (p. 50)
    (a) Only the mean
    (b) Only the median
    * (c) *Both* the mean and the median
    (d) *Neither* the mean nor the median

17. If one score of 8 is changed to 7, which of the following will change? (p. 50)
    * (a) Only the mean
    (b) Only the median
    (c) *Both* the mean and the median
    (d) *Neither* the mean nor the median

18. If one score of 8 is changed to 2, which of the following will change? (p. 50)
    (a) Only the mean
    (b) Only the median
    * (c) *Both* the mean and the median
    (d) *Neither* the mean nor the median

19. If the score of 10 is changed to 1,000,000, what will happen to the mean and the median? (p. 50)
    (a) They will remain the same.
    (b) The median will increase slightly and the mean will increase slightly.
    (a) The median will increase slightly and the mean will increase by a large amount.
    * (d) The median will remain the same and the mean will increase by a large amount.

20. If one score of 8 is changed to 4 *and* one score of 7 is changed to 10, which of the following will change? (p. 50)
    (a) Only the mean
    * (b) Only the median
    (c) *Both* the mean and the median
    (d) *Neither* the mean nor the median

21. If one score of 8 is changed to 7 *and* one score of 3 is changed to 4, (p. 50)
    which of the following will change?
    (a) Only the mean
    (b) Only the median
    (c) *Both* the mean and the median
    * (d) *Neither* the mean nor the median

22. The *mode* for this set of data is equal to: (p. 51)
    (a) 5.0
    (b) 6.0
    (c) 6.5
    * (d) 7.0

Questions 23–34 refer to the set of data shown below:

X	f	cf
10	0	18
9	0	18
8	0	18
7	1	18
6	0	17
5	1	17
4	1	16
3	3	15
2	6	12
1	4	6
0	2	2

23. The *median* divides this set of scores so that: (p. 49)
    * (a) nine scores fall below the median and nine scores fall above the median.
    (b) 10 scores fall below the median and 10 scores fall above the median.
    (c) six scores fall below the median and 12 scores fall above the median.
    (d) two scores fall below the median and eight scores fall above the median.

24. The median of this set of scores is equal to: (p. 49)
    (a) 1.5
    * (b) 2.0
    (c) 2.5
    (d) 3.0

25. The *mean* of this set of scores is equal to: (p. 47)
    (a) 2.00
    * (b) 2.28
    (c) 4.50
    (d) Cannot be determined from the information given

26. A comparison of the mean and median indicates that this set of data is: (p. 50)
    (a) rectangular.
    (b) negatively skewed.
    * (c) positively skewed.
    (d) *none* of the above

27. If the score of 7 is changed to 10, which of the following will change? (p. 50)
    * (a) Only the mean
    (b) Only the median
    (c) *Both* the mean and the median
    (d) *Neither* the mean nor the median

28. If one score of 1 is changed to zero, which of the following will change? (p. 50)
    * (a) Only the mean
    (b) Only the median
    (c) *Both* the mean and the median
    (d) *Neither* the mean nor the median

29. If one score of 1 is changed to 9, which of the following will change? (p. 50)
    (a) Only the mean
    (b) Only the median
    * (c) *Both* the mean and the median
    (d) *Neither* the mean nor the median

30. If the score of 7 is changed to 1, which of the following will change? (p. 50)
    (a) Only the mean
    (b) Only the median
    * (c) *Both* the mean and the median
    (d) *Neither* the mean nor the median

31. If the score of 5 is changed to 4 *and* one score of zero is changed to 1, which of the following will change? (p. 50)
    (a) Only the mean
    (b) Only the median
    (c) *Both* the mean and the median
    * (d) *Neither* the mean nor the median

32. If the score of 7 is changed to 4 *and* one score of 1 is also changed to 4, (p. 50)
    which of the following will change?
    (a) Only the mean
    * (b) Only the median
    (c) *Both* the mean and the median
    (d) *Neither* the mean nor the median

33. If the score of zero is changed to *minus* 1,000,000, what will happen to (p. 50)
    the mean and the median?
    (a) They will remain the same.
    (b) The median will decrease slightly and the mean will decrease slightly.
    (c) The median will decrease slightly and the mean will decrease by a large amount.
    * (d) The median will remain the same and the mean will decrease by a large amount.

34. The *mode* for this set of data is: (p. 51)
    (a) 1.0
    (b) 1.5
    * (c) 2.0
    (d) 2.5

Questions 35–40 refer to the set of data shown below:

X	f	cf
10	1	14
9	1	13
8	2	12
7	5	10
6	2	5
5	0	3
4	0	3
3	0	3
2	1	3
1	0	2
0	2	2

35. The *median* divides this set of scores so that: (p. 49)
    (a) five scores fall below the median and five scores fall above it.
    * (b) seven scores fall below the median and seven scores fall above it.
    (c) five scores fall below the median and nine scores fall above it.
    (d) *none* of the above

36. The median of this set of scores is equal to: (p. 49)
    (a) 6.0
    (b) 6.5
    * (c) 6.9
    (d) 7.5

37. The *mean* of this set of scores is equal to: (p. 47)
    (a) 1.00
    (b) 3.93
    * (c) 6.00
    (d) Cannot be determined from the information given

38. A comparison of the mean and the median indicates that this set of scores is: (p. 50)
    (a) rectangular.
    * (b) negatively skewed.
    (c) positively skewed.
    (d) *none* of the above

39. The *mode* for this set of data is: (p. 51)
    (a) 6.5
    * (b) 7.0
    (c) 7.5
    (d) Cannot be determined from the information given

40. If the value of the highest score is not known exactly, and all we know is (p. 50)
    that it took a rat "more than 10 minutes" to run a maze because the rat
    refused to run at all, which of the following could be computed as a measure
    of central tendency?
    (a) Only the mean
    * (b) Only the median
    (c) *Both* the mean and the median
    (d) *Neither* the mean nor the median

41. In a positively skewed distribution: (p. 50)
    (a) the mean is smaller than the median.
    * (b) the mean is larger than the median.
    (c) the mean and the median are equal.
    (d) *none* of the above

42. In a *negatively skewed* distribution: (p. 50)
    * (a) the mean is smaller than the median.
    (b) the mean is larger than the median.
    (c) the mean and the median are equal.
    (d) *none* of the above

43. In a *symmetric* distribution: (p. 50)
    (a) the mean is smaller than the median.
    (b) the mean is larger than the median.
    * (c) the mean and the median are equal.
    (d) *none* of the above

44. Which of the following is almost never used in the behavioral sciences (p. 51)
    because it is often a poor measure of central tendency?
    (a) The mean
    (b) The median
    * (c) The mode
    (d) *None* of the above

45. Which measure gives the most consistent results when drawing different (p. 48)
    samples from the same population?
    * (a) The mean
    (b) The median
    (c) The mode
    (d) The median if samples are large, and the mean if samples are small

46. Which measure is computed using all of the scores? (p. 48)
    * (a) The mean
    (b) The median
    (c) The mode
    (d) *All* of the above

47. Which measure is the best one to use when the data are highly skewed (p. 50)
    and the purpose is purely descriptive?
    (a) The mean
    * (b) The median
    (c) The mode
    (d) *None* of the above

48. Which measure should be used when there are inexact data at the extremes (p. 50)
    of a distribution, such as "more than 50"?
    (a) The mean
    * (b) The median
    (c) The mode
    (d) *None* of the above

49. From which measure is the sum of the deviations, keeping the sign, (p. 47)
    equal to zero?
    * (a) The mean
    (b) The median
    (c) The mode
    (d) *All* of the above

50. To a group of 25 children with IQs ranging from 82 to 121, (pp. 48, 50, 51)
    a child with an IQ of 143 is added. Which of the following measures
    will change the most?
    * (a) The mean
    (b) The median
    (c) The mode
    (d) None of the measures will change.

Chapter 5

1. The standard deviation and variance are measures of: (pp. 57–58)
    (a) the general location of a set of scores.
    * (b) how spread out the scores in a set of data are from one another.
    (c) *both* of the above
    (d) *neither* of the above

2. Which of the following sets of scores has the *largest* amount of variability? (p. 53)
    (a) 102.7, 103.2, 104.6, 103.5, 100.9, 101.4
    (b) 11, 12, 12, 12, 12, 12, 12, 13
    * (c) 1, 0, 6, 9, 12, 14, 3, 8, 17, 2, 5, 6, 15
    (d) 1,000,000; 1,000,001; 1,000,002; 1,000,004

3. Ten people have exactly the same score. All of them received a score of 4.0. (p. 53)
    The variability of these 10 scores is:
    * (a) zero
    (b) 1.0
    (c) 4.0
    (d) Cannot be determined from the information given

4. Variability can be less than zero (negative). (p. 53)
    (a) True
    * (b) False

5. Which of the following *cannot* be negative? (p. 53)
    (a) The mean
    (b) The median
    (c) The mode
    * (d) The standard deviation

6. If you score above average on a midterm exam, you're more likely to (pp. 53–54)
    get a higher letter grade if the standard deviation is:
    * (a) small.
    (b) medium.
    (c) large.
    (d) cannot be determined from the information given

7. If you score below average on a midterm exam, you're more likely to get (pp. 53–54)
a higher letter grade if the standard deviation is:
   (a) small.
   (b) medium.
   * (c) large.
   (d) cannot be determined from the information given

8. Variability is important to behavioral scientists because: (p. 55)
   (a) it can be measured numerically.
   (b) any variability is due to errors in measurement.
   (c) every test has a standard deviation.
   * (d) human beings differ on important traits and characteristics.

9. A researcher draws five samples of size 50 from the *same* population and (p. 55)
computes the mean of each sample. The researcher is more likely to obtain
an accurate estimate of the population mean if the variability of these five
sample means is:
   * (a) small.
   (b) medium.
   (c) large.
   (d) *none* of the above

10. A researcher who is interested in introversion-extraversion wants to study (p. 54)
the entire range of behavior from extremely introverted to extremely
extraverted. The researcher needs a group of subjects for whom the
variability on introversion-extraversion is:
   (a) small.
   (b) medium.
   * (c) large.
   (d) *none* of the above

11. A researcher is interested in studying gifted children who have an IQ of 130 (p. 54)
or more. As compared to the general population, the variability of the
IQ scores for the group of gifted children is:
   * (a) smaller.
   (b) the same.
   (c) larger.
   (d) cannot be determined from the information given

12. An intelligence test is given to two groups. Group A consists of adults (p. 54)
    chosen at random from the population of American citizens. Group B
    consists of Harvard graduates. The variability of the test scores will be:
    * (a) larger for Group A.
    (b) larger for Group B.
    (c) the same for both groups since the same test is used.
    (d) cannot be determined from the information given

13. Which of the following is almost never used in the behavioral sciences (p. 56)
    because it is often a poor measure of variability?
    (a) The standard deviation
    (b) The variance
    * (c) The range
    (d) *None* of the above

14. Which of the following is computed using all of the scores? (pp. 55, 58)
    (a) The range
    * (b) The standard deviation
    (c) *Both* of the above
    (d) *Neither* of the above

15. The range is defined as: (p. 55)
    (a) the average distance between each pair of scores.
    (b) the average distance of each score from the mean.
    (c) the average distance of each score from the median.
    * (d) the largest score minus the smallest score.

16. Variability refers to the difference between each score and every other score. (p. 56)
    * (a) True
    (b) False

17. The *deviation* of a single score is defined as its difference from: (p. 56)
    (a) every other score.
    * (b) the mean.
    (c) the median.
    (d) *none* of the above

18. The *absolute value* of a score is defined as: (p. 57)
    (a) its distance from the mean.
    (b) its distance from the median.
    (c) the square root of the score.
    * (d) its numerical value ignoring the sign.

19. Why can't the sum of the deviations from the mean for all of the scores be used as a measure of variability? (p. 57)
    (a) It is in the wrong unit of measurement.
    (b) It will overestimate the variability of the set of scores.
    (c) Deviations from the mean have no effect on variability.
    * (d) It is always equal to zero.

20. If the variability of a set of scores is large: (p. 56)
    * (a) many of the scores will have large deviations from the mean.
    (b) most of the scores will be close to the mean.
    (c) the sum of deviations from the mean will be large.
    (d) the sum of deviations from the mean will be small.

21. If the variability of a set of scores is small: (p. 56)
    (a) many of the scores will have large deviations from the mean.
    * (b) most of the scores will be close to the mean.
    (c) the sum of deviations from the mean will be large.
    (d) the sum of deviations from the mean will be small.

22. If we subtract the mean from each score and then square each of the results, we obtain the: (p. 57)
    (a) standard deviation.
    (b) variance.
    * (c) sum of squares.
    (d) range.

23. If we subtract the mean from each score, square each of the results, and then divide by the number of scores, we obtain the: (p. 57)
    (a) standard deviation.
    * (b) variance.
    (c) sum of squares.
    (d) range.

24. If we subtract the mean from each score, square each of the results, divide by the number of scores, and then take the square root, we obtain the: (p. 58)
    * (a) standard deviation.
    (b) variance.
    (c) sum of squares.
    (d) range.

25. If we divide the sum of squares by the number of scores, we obtain the: (p. 57)
    (a) standard deviation.
    * (b) variance.
    (c) range.
    (d) *none* of the above

26. If we divide the sum of squares by the number of scores and then take the square root, we obtain the: (p. 58)
    * (a) standard deviation.
    (b) variance.
    (c) range.
    (d) *none* of the above

27. When we wish to estimate the variance of a population based on data obtained from a sample, we divide the sum of squares by: (p. 57)
    (a) N.
    * (b) N – 1.
    (c) N – 2.
    (d) *None* of the above

28. A teacher wishes to compute the standard deviation of a midterm exam. The teacher is interested in only this class and does *not* wish to draw inferences about any population. The sum of squares should be divided by: (p. 57)
    * (a) N.
    (b) N – 1.
    (c) N – 2.
    (d) *None* of the above

29. When computing the standard deviation, the last step is to take the square root. This is done to: (p. 58)
    (a) prevent the result from always being zero.
    * (b) return to the original unit of measurement.
    (c) provide a more accurate estimate of the population.
    (d) *all* of the above

30. When computing the variance or standard deviation, all of the deviations from the mean are squared. This is done to: (p. 57)
    * (a) prevent the result from always being zero.
    (b) return to the original unit of measurement.
    (c) provide a more accurate estimate of the population.
    (d) *all* of the above

31. The *variance* is: (p. 58)
    (a) a measure of central tendency.
    (b) the square root of the standard deviation.
    * (c) the square of the standard deviation.
    (d) *none* of the above

Questions 32–37 refer to the set of data shown below:

Quiz Scores: 7, 5, 4, 2, 2   (Mean = 4.0)

32. If we do not wish to estimate a population value, the *variance* of these five scores is: (p. 57)
    (a) the square root of 3.6.
    * (b) 3.6.
    (c) the square root of 4.5.
    (d) 4.5.

33. If we do *not* wish to estimate a population value, the *standard deviation* of these five scores is: (p. 58)
    * (a) the square root of 3.6.
    (b) 3.6.
    (c) the square root of 4.5.
    (d) 4.5.

34. If we wish to estimate the variability of the population from which these five cases were drawn, the *variance* is equal to: (p. 57)
    (a) the square root of 3.6.
    (b) 3.6.
    (c) the square root of 4.5.
    * (d) 4.5.

35. If we wish to estimate the variability of the population from which these five cases were drawn, the *standard deviation* is: (p. 58)
    (a) the square root of 3.6.
    (b) 3.6.
    * (c) the square root of 4.5.
    (d) 4.5.

36. If the score of 7 is changed to 42, the standard deviation will: (p. 58)
    (a) become smaller.
    (b) remain the same.
    * (c) become larger.
    (d) cannot be determined from the information given

37. If the score of 7 is changed to 5 and one score of 2 is changed to 4, (p. 58)
the standard deviation will:
* (a) become smaller.
  (b) remain the same.
  (c) become larger.
  (d) cannot be determined from the information given

Questions 38–44 refer to the set of data shown below:

X	f
5	3
4	1
3	3
2	1
1	0
0	2

Mean = 3.0

38. The *sum of squares* for this set of scores is equal to: (p. 57)
   (a) 15
   (b) 24
* (c) 32
   (d) *none* of the above

39. If we do *not* wish to estimate a population value, the variance and standard (p. 57)
deviation are computed by dividing by:
   (a) 5
   (b) 6
   (c) 9
* (d) 10

40. If we wish to estimate the variability of the population from which these cases (p. 57)
were drawn, the variance and standard deviation are computed by dividing by:
   (a) 5
   (b) 6
* (c) 9
   (d) 10

41. If we do *not* wish to estimate a population value, the *standard deviation* of this set of scores is equal to: (p. 58)
    (a) 1.55
    (b) 1.63
    * (c) 1.79
    (d) 1.89

42. If we wish to estimate the variability of the population from which these cases were drawn, the *standard deviation* of this set of scores is equal to: (p. 58)
    (a) 1.55
    (b) 1.63
    (c) 1.79
    * (d) 1.89

43. If one score of 5 is changed to 15, the standard deviation will: (p. 57)
    (a) become smaller.
    (b) remain the same.
    * (c) become larger.
    (d) cannot be determined from the information given

44. If the score of 4 is changed to 3 and the score of 2 is changed to 3, the standard deviation will: (p. 58)
    * (a) become smaller.
    (b) remain the same.
    (c) become larger.
    (d) cannot be determined from the information given

Questions 45–51 refer to the two sets of data shown below:

X	f	Y	f
10	1	10	1
9	0	9	1
8	0	8	0
7	0	7	1
6	3	6	2
5	2	5	1
4	3	4	1
3	0	3	0
2	0	2	1
1	0	1	1
0	1	0	1

Mean = 5.0   Mean = 5.0

45. The variability of the X scores is: (p. 53)
    (a) greater than the variability of the Y scores.
    (b) equal to the variability of the Y scores.
    * (c) less than the variability of the Y scores.

46. The *range* of the X scores is: (p. 55)
    (a) greater than the range of the Y scores.
    * (b) equal to the range of the Y scores.
    (c) less than the range of the Y scores.
    (d) cannot be determined from the information given

47. What are the *sums of squares* of the X scores and the Y scores? (p. 57)
    (a) $SS_X = 110$, $SS_Y = 110$
    (b) $SS_X = 52$, $SS_Y = 97$
    (c) $SS_X = 60$, $SS_Y = 42$
    * (d) $SS_X = 56$, $SS_Y = 98$

48. If we do *not* wish to estimate any population values, the *standard deviations* (p. 58)
    of the X scores and the Y scores are equal to:
    (a) X: 3.31, Y: 3.31
    (b) X: 2.28, Y: 3.11
    * (c) X: 2.37, Y: 3.13
    (d) X: 2.49, Y: 3.30

49. If we wish to estimate the variability in the populations from which each set (p. 58)
    of data was drawn, the *standard deviations* of the X scores and the Y scores
    are equal to:
    (a) X: 3.50; Y: 3.50
    (b) X: 2.40; Y: 3.28
    (c) X: 2.37; Y: 3.13
    * (d) X: 2.49; Y: 3.30

50. If we wish to estimate the variability in the populations from which each set of (p. 57)
    data was drawn, the variance and the standard deviation are computed by
    dividing each sum of squares by:
    * (a) 9
    (b) 10
    (c) 11
    (d) Cannot be determined from the information given

51. If we do not wish to estimate any population values, the variance and standard deviation for each set of data are computed by dividing each sum of squares by: (p. 57)
   (a) 9
* (b) 10
   (c) 11
   (d) Cannot be determined from the information given

Chapter 6

1. *ALL* of the following are *transformed scores* EXCEPT: (pp. 69, 72, 73)
    (a) an SAT score of 530.
    (b) a T score of 47.
    (c) a Z score of 0.75.
    * (d) a score of 7 on a 10-point quiz.

2. Which of the following is a *raw score*? (pp. 69, 72, 73)
    (a) An SAT score of 460
    (b) A T score of 61
    (c) A Z score of –1.42
    * (d) A score of 76 on a 100-point midterm exam

3. SAT scores, T scores, and Z scores build what information into the score itself? (pp. 69, 72, 73)
    * (a) The mean and standard deviation
    (b) The median and standard deviation
    (c) Only the mean
    (4) Only the standard deviation

4. Which of the following represents the highest score? (pp. 69, 72, 73)
    (a) An SAT score of 580
    (b) A T score of 61
    * (c) A Z score of +1.47
    (d) They are equal

5. Which of the following represents the lowest score? (pp. 69, 72, 73)
    * (a) An SAT score of 360
    (b) A T score of 41
    (c) A Z score of –0.57
    (d) They are equal

6. Which of the following represents the highest score? (pp. 69, 72, 73)
    (a) An SAT score of 620
    (b) A T score of 62
    (c) A Z score of +1.20
    * (d) They are equal

7. Which of the following represents the lowest score? (pp. 69, 72, 73)
   (a) An SAT score of 360
   (b) A T score of 36
   (c) A Z score of −1.40
   * (d) They are equal

8. Which of the following represents the highest score? (pp. 69, 72, 73)
   (a) An SAT score of 710
   * (b) A T score of 72
   (c) A Z score of +2.00
   (d) They are equal

9. Which of the following represents the lowest score? (pp. 69, 72, 73)
   (a) An SAT score of 410
   * (b) A T score of 40
   (c) A Z score of −0.44
   (d) They are equal

10. A set of scores has a mean of 5.3 and a standard deviation of 1.6. If 4 points (p. 67)
    are added to each score, what are the new mean and standard deviation?
    (a) Mean = 5.3, standard deviation = 1.6
    * (b) Mean = 9.3, standard deviation = 1.6
    (c) Mean = 5.3, standard deviation = 5.6
    (d) Mean = 9.3, standard deviation = 5.6

11. A set of scores has a mean of 23.8 and a standard deviation of 4.2. If 3 points (p. 67)
    are subtracted from each score, what are the new mean and standard deviation?
    (a) Mean = 23.8, standard deviation = 4.2
    * (b) Mean = 20.8, standard deviation = 4.2
    (c) Mean = 23.8, standard deviation = 1.2
    (d) Mean = 20.8, standard deviation = 1.2

12. A set of scores has a mean of 7.0 and a standard deviation of 3.2. If every (p. 67)
    score is multiplied by 2, what are the new mean and standard deviation?
    (a) Mean = 7.0, standard deviation = 3.2
    (b) Mean = 14.0, standard deviation = 3.2
    (c) Mean = 7.0, standard deviation 6.4
    * (d) Mean = 14.0, standard deviation = 6.4

13. A set of scores has a mean of 10.5 and a standard deviation of 3.5. If every (p. 67)
    score is divided by 5, what are the new mean and standard deviation?
    (a) Mean = 10.5, standard deviation = 3.5
    (b) Mean = 2.1, standard deviation = 3.5
    (c) Mean = 10.5, standard deviation = 0.7
    * (d) Mean = 2.1, standard deviation 0.7

14. If the standard deviation of a set of scores is 4.0 and each score is multiplied (p. 67)
    by 3, what is the new *variance*?
    (a) 4.0
    (b) 12.0
    (c) 27.0
    * (d) 144.0

15. A set of scores has a mean of 27.4 and a standard deviation of 4.6. If 27.4 (p. 67)
    is subtracted from each score, what are the new mean and standard deviation?
    (a) Mean = 27.4, standard deviation = 4.6
    * (b) Mean = 0, standard deviation = 4.6
    (c) Mean = 27.4, standard deviation = −22.8
    (d) Mean = 0, standard deviation = −22.8

16. A set of scores has a mean of 0 and a standard deviation of 1. If each score (p. 67)
    is multiplied by 10, what are the new mean and standard deviation?
    (a) Mean = 0, standard deviation = 1
    * (b) Mean = 0, standard deviation = 10
    (c) Mean = 10, standard deviation = 1
    (d) Mean = 10, standard deviation = 10

17. A set of scores has a mean of 15.3 and a standard deviation of 3.0. If we (p. 67)
    first subtract 15.3 from every score and then divide each of the new scores
    by 3.0, what are the new mean and standard deviation?
    (a) Mean = 5.1, standard deviation = 3.0
    (b) Mean = 0, standard deviation = 3.0
    * (c) Mean = 0, standard deviation = 1
    (d) Mean = 5.1, standard deviation = 1

18. The mean of a set of Z scores is equal to: (p. 69)
    (a) −1.00.
    * (b) 0.
    (c) 1.00.
    (d) the standard deviation of the raw scores.

19. The standard deviation of a set of Z scores is equal to: (p. 69)
    (a) −1.00.
    (b) 0.
    * (c) +1.00.
    (d) the number of scores (N).

20. What are the mean and standard deviation of a set of T scores? (p. 72)
    (a) Mean = 0, standard deviation = 1
    (b) Mean = 10, standard deviation = 1
    * (c) Mean = 50, standard deviation = 10
    (d) Mean = 500, standard deviation = 100

21. What are the mean and standard deviation of a set of SAT scones? (p. 73)
    (a) Mean = 0, standard deviation = 1
    (b) Mean = 10, standard deviation = 1
    (c) Mean = 50, standard deviation = 10
    * (d) Mean = 500, standard deviation = 100

22. A frequency distribution contains 40 scores that vary from 124 to 197. If we (p. 67)
    subtract 100 from each score, which of the following will *NOT* change?
    (a) The mean
    (b) The median
    (c) The mode
    * (d) The standard deviation

23. If we convert a set of raw scores to Z scores, the *shape* of the distribution will: (p. 71)
    (a) become more symmetric.
    (b) become more skewed.
    (c) become more like the bell-shaped normal curve.
    * (d) remain the same.

24. On a midterm exam, your score expressed as a Z score is +0.50. The mean (p. 69)
    of the exam is 65 and the standard deviation is 10. Your raw score is:
    (a) 60
    (b) 65
    * (c) 70
    (d) 75

25. On a midterm exam, your score expressed as a Z score is −1.50. The mean (p. 69)
   of the exam is 70 and the standard deviation is 8. Your raw score is:
   (a) 54
   * (b) 58
   (c) 82
   (d) 86

26. On a midterm exam, your score expressed as a T score is 62. The mean (p. 72)
   of the exam is 72 and the standard deviation is 5. Your raw score is:
   (a) 66
   (b) 67
   (c) 77
   * (d) 78

27. On a midterm exam, your score expressed as a T score is 40. The mean (p. 72)
   of the exam is 75 and the standard deviation is 7. Your raw score is:
   (a) 61
   * (b) 68
   (c) 82
   (d) 89

28. On a midterm exam, your score expressed as an SAT score is 550. The mean (p. 73)
   of the exam is 74 and the standard deviation is 6. Your raw score is:
   (a) 68
   (b) 71
   * (c) 77
   (d) 80

29. On a midterm exam, your score expressed as an SAT score is 300. The mean (p. 73)
   of the exam is 70 and the standard deviation is 8. Your raw score is:
   * (a) 54
   (b) 58
   (c) 62
   (d) 78

30. A Z score of +2.00 is equal to: (pp. 69, 72, 73)
   (a) a T score of 20.
   * (b) an SAT score of 700.
   (c) a raw score of 90 on a test with a mean of 75 and a standard deviation of 15.
   (d) *all* of the above
   (e) *none* of the above

31. A Z score of –1.50 is equal to: (pp. 69, 72, 73)
    (a) a T score of 30.
    (b) an SAT score of 400.
    * (c) a raw score of 67 on a test with a mean of 76 and a standard deviation of 6.
    (d) *all* of the above
    (e) *none* of the above

32. A Z score of 0 is equal to: (pp. 69, 72, 73)
    (a) a T score of 0.
    (b) a score of 0 on a quiz with a mean of 5.3 and a standard deviation of 10.
    * (c) a score of 72 on a test with a mean of 72 and a standard deviation of 6.4.
    (d) *all* of the above
    (e) *none* of the above

33. A Z score of 0 is equal to: (pp. 69, 72, 73)
    (a) a T score of 50.
    (b) an SAT score of 500.
    (c) a score of 75 on a test with a mean of 75.
    * (d) *all* of the above
    (e) *none* of the above

34. A Z score of 0 is equal to: (pp. 69, 72, 73)
    (a) a T score of 0.
    (b) an SAT score of 0.
    (c) a score of 0 on a quiz with a mean of 5.0.
    (d) *all* of the above
    * (e) *none* of the above

35. If a student obtains a *negative* Z score: (pp. 69, 72, 73)
    (a) the corresponding T score must be below 50.
    (b) the corresponding SAT score must be below 500.
    (c) the corresponding raw score must be below the mean.
    * (d) *all* of the above
    (e) *none* of the above

36. If a student obtains a *negative* Z score: (pp. 69, 72, 73)
    (a) the corresponding T score must be negative.
    (b) the corresponding SAT score must be below 400.
    * (c) the corresponding raw score must be below the mean.
    (d) *all* of the above
    (e) *none* of the above

37. If we transform a set of raw scores to Z scores and plot the Z scores as (p. 71)
    a regular frequency polygon, the shape of the distribution will be the
    bell-shaped normal curve:
    (a) always—graphing a set of Z scores always produces the bell-shaped normal curve.
    * (b) only if the distribution of raw scores was also the bell-shaped normal curve.
    (c) never—a set of Z scores cannot take the form of the bell-shaped normal curve.

38. If we have a set of Z scores and we add 3 points to each score, what are (pp. 67, 69)
    the new mean and standard deviation?
    (a) Mean = 0, standard deviation = 1
    * (b) Mean = 3, standard deviation = 1
    (c) Mean = 3, standard deviation = 4
    (d) Cannot be determined from the information given

39. It is mathematically possible, but very unlikely, to obtain a Z score of –3.00 (p. 72)
    or less or +3.00 or more.
    * (a) True
    (b) False

Questions 40–50 refer to a set of data where:

$$\text{Mean} = 67.0$$
$$\text{Standard deviation} = 4.0$$

40. A raw score of 72 is equal to a Z score of: (p. 69)
    (a) –1.00
    (b) +1.00
    * (c) +1.25
    (d) +1.50

41. A raw score of 60 is equal to a Z score of: (p. 69)
    (a) –2.00
    (b) –1.75
    (c) –1.60
    (d) –1.50

42. A raw score of 77 is equal to a Z score of: (p. 69)
    (a) –2.00
    (b) +2.00
    (c) +2.25
    * (d) +2.50

54 ✦ CHAPTER 6

43. Converting a raw score of 77 to a Z score shows that if this is a midterm (p. 69)
    exam, the score of 77 will receive a grade of:
    * (a) A
    (b) B
    (c) C
    (d) Below C

44. The highest score in this set of data is most likely to be: (p. 72)
    (a) 70
    * (b) 75
    (c) 90
    (d) 95

45. A Z score of –0.75 is equal to a raw score of: (p. 69)
    (a) 63
    * (b) 64
    (c) 70
    (d) 71

46. A Z score of +0.50 is equal to a raw score of: (p. 69)
    (a) 63
    (b) 65
    * (c) 69
    (d) 70

47. A raw score of 69 is equal to a T score of: (p. 72)
    (a) 45
    (b) 50
    * (c) 55
    (d) 60

48. A raw score of 59 is equal to a T score of: (p. 72)
    * (a) 30
    (b) 35
    (c) 40
    (d) 45

49. A raw score of 67 is equal to an SAT score of: (p. 73)
    (a) 400
    (b) 450
    * (c) 500
    (d) 550

Harcourt, Inc.

50. A raw score of 74 is equal to an SAT score of: (p. 73)
    (a) 650
    * (b) 675
    (c) 700
    (d) 725

Questions 51–60 refer to a midterm exam with a mean of 76.0 and a standard deviation of 8.0.

51. Any student with a Z score of +1.50 or higher will receive a grade of A. (p. 69)
    The minimum raw score needed to receive an A is:
    (a) 84
    (b) 86
    * (c) 88
    (d) 90

52. Students with Z scores between +0.50 and +1.50 will receive a grade of B. (p. 69)
    To receive a B, a student's raw score must be between:
    (a) 80 and 90
    * (b) 80 and 88
    (c) 84 and 90
    (d) 84 and 88

53. Students with Z scores between −1.00 and +0.50 will receive a grade of C. (p. 69)
    To receive a C, a student's raw score must be between:
    (a) 72 and 80
    (b) 72 and 84
    (c) 68 and 84
    * (d) 68 and 80

54. Any student with a Z score of −2.00 or less will receive a grade of F. (p. 69)
    To receive an F, a student's raw score must be:
    (a) 68 or less
    (b) 64 or less
    * (c) 60 or less
    (d) 56 or less

55. A student with a Z score of zero will receive a grade of: (p. 69)
    (a) A
    (b) B
    * (c) C
    (d) F

56. If only those students with SAT scores of 700 or higher will receive a grade (p. 73)
    of A, the minimum raw score needed to receive an A is:
    (a) 84
    (b) 88
    (c) 90
    * (d) 92

57. To pass the exam, a student must obtain an SAT score of at least 350. (p. 73)
    The minimum passing raw score is:
    (a) 60
    * (b) 64
    (c) 66
    (d) 68

58. To receive a grade of B, a student must have a T score between 55 and 60. (p. 72)
    What raw scores will receive a grade of B?
    (a) Between 78 and 88
    (b) Between 80 and 88
    * (c) Between 80 and 84
    (d) Between 78 and 84

59. Students with T scores between 35 and 55 will receive a grade of C. (p. 72)
    To receive a C, a student's raw score must be between:
    (a) 64 and 84
    (b) 72 and 80
    * (c) 64 and 80
    (d) 72 and 84

60. The teacher calculates a student's Z score as +4.62. The most likely (p. 72)
    interpretation of this score is:
    (a) the student received the highest score in the class.
    (b) the student deserves a grade of B.
    (c) the distribution of test scores was negatively skewed.
    * (d) the teacher made an error in calculation.

Chapter 7

1. Transformed scores such as Z, T, and SAT are more likely to give *misleading* (p. 77)
   results if the distribution of scores is:
   - (a) unimodal and bell-shaped.
   - (b) unimodal and symmetric.
   - (c) bimodal and symmetric.
   - * (d) highly skewed.

Questions 2–15 refer to the two five-number summaries shown below:

	Summary 1			Summary 2	
	32			31	
24		37	26		35
11		51	10		50

2. In Summary 1, the score corresponding to the first quartile is: (p. 78)
   - (a) 11
   - * (b) 24
   - (c) 32
   - (d) 37

3. In Summary 1, the score corresponding to the third quartile is: (p. 78)
   - (a) 11
   - (b) 24
   - (c) 32
   - * (d) 37

4. In Summary 1, the score corresponding to the median is: (p. 78)
   - (a) 11
   - (b) 24
   - * (c) 32
   - (d) 37

5. In Summary 1, the score of 11 represents: (p. 78)
   - (a) the score corresponding to the 5th percentile.
   - (b) the score corresponding to the 10th percentile.
   - (c) the score corresponding to the 25th percentile.
   - * (d) the lowest score.

6. In Summary 1, the score of 51 represents: (p. 78)
   (a) the score corresponding to the median.
   (b) the score corresponding to the 75th percentile.
   (c) the score corresponding to the 90th percentile.
   * (d) the highest score.

7. In Summary 2, the score corresponding to the first quartile is: (p. 78)
   (a) 10
   * (b) 26
   (c) 31
   (d) 35

8. In Summary 2, the score corresponding to the third quartile is: (p. 78)
   (a) 10
   (b) 26
   (c) 31
   * (d) 35

9. In Summary 2, the score corresponding to the median is: (p. 78)
   (a) 10
   (b) 26
   * (c) 31
   (d) 35

10. In Summary 2, the score of 10 represents: (p. 78)
    (a) the score corresponding to the 5th percentile.
    (b) the score corresponding to the 10th percentile.
    (c) the score corresponding to the 25th percentile.
    * (d) the lowest score.

11. In Summary 2, the score of 50 represents: (p. 78)
    (a) the score corresponding to the median.
    (b) the score corresponding to the 75th percentile.
    (c) the score corresponding to the 90th percentile.
    * (d) the highest score.

12. Summary 1 shows that the distribution of this set of scores is: (p. 78)
    (a) symmetric but not bell-shaped.
    (b) symmetric and bell-shaped.
    (c) bimodal.
    * (d) skewed.

13. Distribution 1 is: (p. 79)
    * (a) less symmetric than distribution 2.
    (b) equal in symmetry to distribution 2.
    (c) more symmetric than distribution 2.
    (d) cannot be determined from the information given

14. Distribution 1 is: (p. 79)
    (a) less variable than distribution 2.
    (b) equal in variability to distribution 2.
    * (c) more variable than distribution 2.
    (d) cannot be determined from the information given

15. The location of distribution 1 is: (p. 79)
    (a) 10 points lower than that of distribution 2.
    * (b) about the same as that of distribution 2.
    (c) 10 points higher than that of distribution 2.
    (d) cannot be determined from the information given

Questions 16–29 refer to the two five-number summaries shown below:

	Summary X			Summary Y	
	25			35	
20		29	27		40
4		44	14		54

16. In Summary X, the score corresponding to the first quartile is: (p. 78)
    * (a) 20
    (b) 25
    (c) 29
    (d) 44

17. In Summary X, the score corresponding to the third quartile is: (p. 78)
    (a) 20
    (b) 25
    * (c) 29
    (d) 44

18. In Summary X, the score corresponding to the median is: (p. 78)
    (a) 20
    * (b) 25
    (c) 29
    (d) 44

19. In Summary X, the score of 4 represents: (p. 78)
    (a) the score corresponding to the 5th percentile.
    (b) the score corresponding to the 10th percentile.
    (c) the score corresponding to the 25th percentile.
    * (d) the lowest score.

20. In Summary X, the score of 44 represents: (p. 78)
    (a) the score corresponding to the median.
    (b) the score corresponding to the 75th percentile.
    (c) the score corresponding to the 90th percentile.
    * (d) the highest score.

21. In Summary Y, the score corresponding to the first quartile is: (p. 78)
    * (a) 27
    (b) 35
    (c) 40
    (d) 54

22. In Summary Y, the score corresponding to the third quartile is: (p. 78)
    (a) 27
    (b) 35
    * (c) 40
    (d) 54

23. In Summary Y, the score corresponding to the median is: (p. 78)
    (a) 27
    * (b) 35
    (c) 40
    (d) 54

24. In Summary Y, the score of 14 represents: (p. 78)
    (a) the score corresponding to the 5th percentile.
    (b) the score corresponding to the 10th percentile.
    (c) the score corresponding to the 25th percentile.
    * (d) the lowest score.

25. In Summary Y, the score of 54 represents: (p. 78)
    (a) the score corresponding to the median.
    (b) the score corresponding to the 75th percentile.
    (c) the score corresponding to the 90th percentile.
    * (d) the highest score.

26. Summary Y shows that the distribution of this set of scores is: (p. 79)
    (a) symmetric but not bell-shaped.
    (b) symmetric and bell-shaped.
    * (c) skewed.
    (d) bimodal.

27. Distribution X is: (p. 79)
    (a) less symmetric than distribution Y.
    (b) equal in symmetry to distribution Y.
    * (c) more symmetric than distribution Y.
    (d) cannot be determined from the information given

28. Distribution X is: (p. 79)
    * (a) less variable than distribution Y.
    (b) equal in variability to distribution Y.
    (c) more variable than distribution Y.
    (d) cannot be determined from the information given

29. The location of distribution X is: (p. 79)
    * (a) 10 points lower than that of distribution Y.
    (b) about the same as that of distribution Y.
    (c) 10 points higher than that of distribution Y.
    (d) cannot be determined from the information given

30. The five-number summary is also used in: (pp. 80, 81)
    * (a) box-and-whisker plots.
    (b) mean-on-spoke representations.
    (c) *both* of the above
    (d) *neither* of the above

31. For a bell-shaped distribution, which of the following should be used? (p. 80)
    (a) A box-and-whisker plot
    * (b) A mean-on-spoke representation
    (c) *Both* of the above are equally desirable.
    (d) *Neither* of the above should be used.

Questions 32–35 refer to the mean-on-spoke representations whose numerical values are summarized below.

$$\text{Group 1:} \quad 76 \pm 10$$
$$\text{Group 2:} \quad 74 \pm 11$$
$$\text{Group 3:} \quad 84 \pm 7$$

32. Which group had the highest mean? (p. 81)
    (a) Group 1
    (b) Group 2
    * (c) Group 3
    (d) Cannot be determined from the information given

33. Which group had the smallest variability? (p. 81)
    (a) Group 1
    (b) Group 2
    * (c) Group 3
    (d) Cannot be determined from the information given

34. If the distribution of scores in Group 2 is bell-shaped, about how many of the scores fall between 63 and 85? (p. 81)
    (a) Half of the scores
    * (b) Two-thirds of the scores
    (c) 90 percent of the scores
    (d) 95 percent of the scores

35. If the distribution of scores in Group 1 is bell-shaped, about how many of the scores fall above 86? (p. 81)
    (a) 5 percent
    (b) 10 percent
    * (c) One third of the scores
    (d) Half of the scores

Questions 36–39 refer to the mean-on-spoke representations whose numerical values are summarized below: (p. 81)

$$\text{Group A:} \quad 57 \pm 4$$
$$\text{Group B:} \quad 62 \pm 11$$
$$\text{Group C:} \quad 54 \pm 6$$

36. Which group had the highest mean? (p. 81)
    (a) Group A
    * (b) Group B
    (c) Group C
    (d) Cannot be determined from the information given

37. Which group had the smallest variability? (p. 81)
    * (a) Group A
    (b) Group B
    (c) Group C
    (d) Cannot be determined from the information given

38. If the distribution of scores in Group A is bell-shaped, about how many scores fall between 53 and 61? (p. 81)
    (a) 10 percent of the scores
    (b) 25 percent of the scores
    (c) Half of the scores
    * (d) Two-thirds of the scores

39. If the distribution of scores in Group C is bell-shaped, about how many of the scores fall above 60? (p. 81)
    (a) 10 percent
    (b) 25 percent
    * (c) One third
    (d) One half

40. Which of the following can be used to draw inferences about a population, based on data obtained from a sample? (pp. 81–82)
    (a) Box-and-whisker plots
    (b) Five-number summaries
    (c) Mean-on-spoke representations
    (d) *All* of the above
    * (e) *None* of the above

Chapter 8

1. Why do behavioral scientists use inferential statistics? (p. 88)
   - (a) To summarize important characteristics of a set of data
   - * (b) To draw conclusions about a population that is too large to measure
   - (c) To reduce the amount of error in tests, questionnaires, and other instruments
   - (d) To make accurate inferences about the samples they are studying

2. Behavioral scientists need inferential statistics because: (p. 88)
   - (a) the populations they wish to study are too large to measure.
   - (b) no matter how carefully a sample is drawn, it may *not* accurately reflect what is happening in the population.
   - * (c) *both* of the above
   - (d) *neither* of the above

3. Usually, behavioral scientists are able to measure: (p. 88)
   - (a) the entire population.
   - (b) approximately 75 to 90 percent of the population.
   - (c) at least half of the population.
   - * (d) much less than half of the population.

4. Based on a sample mean, we wish to estimate the value of the population mean. This is called: (p. 89)
   - (a) an interval estimate.
   - * (b) a point estimate.
   - (c) a probability estimate.
   - (d) a statistical estimate.

5. We wish to determine the likelihood that the population mean falls between 72.5 and 88.5. This is called: (p. 89)
   - * (a) an interval estimate.
   - (b) a point estimate.
   - (c) a probability estimate.
   - (d) a statistical estimate.

6. *Probability* is defined as: (p. 91)
    (a) how often the event occurs.
    * (b) the number of ways a specified event can occur divided by the total number of possible events.
    (c) the number of favorable events divided by the number of unfavorable events.
    (d) the number of unfavorable events divided by the number of favorable events.

7. If a six-sided die contains the numbers from 1 to 6, the probability of obtaining a 3 on one throw of the die is: (p. 91)
    (a) 1/2
    (b) 1/3
    (c) 1/5
    * (d) 1/6

8. If a six-sided die contains the numbers from 1 to 6, the *odds against* obtaining a 4 on one throw of the die are: (p. 92)
    (a) 2 to 1
    (b) 4 to 1
    * (c) 5 to 1
    (d) 6 to 1

9. If a six-sided die contains the numbers from 1 to 6, the probability of obtaining *either* a 1 or a 6 on one throw of the die is: (p. 92)
    (a) 1/2
    * (b) 1/3
    (c) 1/4
    (d) 1/6

10. If a six-sided die contains the numbers from 1 to 6, the *odds against* obtaining an even number (2, 4, or 6) on one throw of the die are: (p. 92)
    (a) 1 to 1
    (b) 2 to 1
    (c) 3 to 1
    (d) 6 to 1

11. If a six-sided die contains the numbers from 1 to 6, the probability of obtaining *either* a 1, 2, 3, or 4 on one throw of the die is: (p. 92)
    (a) 1/6
    (b) 1/3
    (c) 1/2
    * (d) 2/3

12. If a six-sided die contains the numbers from 1 to 6, the *odds against* (p. 92)
    obtaining a 4 or a 5 on one throw of the die are:
    (a) 1 to 1
    * (b) 2 to 1
    (c) 3 to 1
    (d) 6 to 1

13. If a six-sided die contains the numbers from 1 to 6, the probability of (p. 92)
    obtaining *either* a 1, 2, 3, 4, 5, or 6 on one throw of the die is:
    (a) 0
    (b) 1/6
    (c) 2/3
    * (d) 1

14. If a six-sided die contains the numbers from 1 to 6, the probability of (p. 92)
    obtaining a 7 on one throw of the die is:
    * (a) 0
    (b) 1/6
    (c) 2/3
    (d) 1

15. The lowest and highest possible values of the probability of an event are: (p. 92)
    (a) minus infinity and plus infinity.
    (b) −1 and +1.
    (c) −1 and 0.
    * (d) 0 and +1.

16. If a coin is flipped twice, the probability of obtaining two beads is: (p. 93)
    (a) 0
    * (b) 1/4
    (c) 1/2
    (d) 1

17. If a coin is flipped twice, the probability of obtaining one head and one (p. 93)
    tail regardless of the order in which these results occur is:
    (a) 0
    (b) 1/4
    * (c) 1/2
    (d) 1

18. If a coin is flipped twice, the probability of obtaining a head on the first flip and a tail on the second flip is: (p. 93)
    (a) 0
    * (b) 1/4
    (c) 1/2
    (d) 1

19. If a six-sided die contains the numbers from 1 to 6, the probability of obtaining a 3 on the first throw and a 4 on the second throw is: (p. 93)
    (a) 1/6
    (b) 1/3
    (c) 1/12
    * (d) 1/36

20. If a six-sided die contains the numbers from 1 to 6 and the die is thrown twice, the following results will produce a sum of 7: 1 and then 6, 2 and then 5, 3 and then 4, 4 and then 3, 5 and then 2, 6 and then 1. What is the probability of obtaining a sum of 7 on two throws of the die? (p. 93)
    * (a) 1/6
    (b) 1/3
    (c) 1/12
    (d) 1/2

21. If a six-sided die contains the numbers from 1 to 6 and the die is thrown twice, what is the probability of obtaining either a 1 or a 2 on the first throw and *then* a 5 on the second throw? (pp. 92–93)
    (a) 1/6 × 1/6
    * (b) 1/3 × 1/6
    (c) 1/6 + 1/6
    (d) 1/3 + 1/6

22. If a six-sided die contains the numbers from 1 to 6 and the die is thrown twice, what is the probability of obtaining an even number on the first throw (2, 4, or 6) and an odd number on the second throw (1, 3, or 5)? (pp. 92–93)
    * (a) 1/2 × 1/2
    (b) 1/3 × 1/3
    (c) 1/2 + 1/2
    (d) 1/3 + 1/3

23. When we compute the probability of obtaining the results of throwing one (p. 95)
    die, we assume that the die is fair—that is, each of the numbers from
    1 to 6 has an equal chance of occurring.
    * (a) True
      (b) False

24. Suppose that a six-sided die containing the numbers from 1 to 6 is "loaded": (p. 95)
    Certain numbers are more likely to occur than others. What is the probability
    of obtaining a 4 on one throw of the die?
      (a) 1/6
      (b) 1/3
      (c) 1/2
    * (d) Cannot be determined from the information given

25. When we compute the probability of obtaining a head or a tail in one flip (p. 95)
    of a coin, we assume that the coin is fair—that is, a head or a tail has an
    equal chance of occurring.
    * (a) True
      (b) False

26. Suppose that a coin is "loaded": a head is more likely to occur on one flip (p. 95)
    of the coin. What is the probability of obtaining a tail on one flip?
      (a) 1/3
      (b) 1/2
      (c) 2/3
    * (d) Cannot be determined from the information given

27. What is the probability of drawing *either* the ace of spades *or* the ten (pp. 92–93)
    of clubs from a standard deck?
      (a) 1/52
    * (b) 1/26
      (c) 8/52
      (d) 1/2

28. What is the probability of drawing *either* the ace of spades *or* a heart (pp. 92–93)
    from a standard deck?
      (a) 1/52
      (b) 2/52
    * (c) 14/52
      (d) 26/52

29. What is the probability of drawing *either* an ace *or* a heart from a (pp. 92–93)
    standard deck?
    (a) 1/52
    (b) 14/52
    * (c) 16/52
    (d) 17/52

30. A card is drawn from a standard deck. Before the next draw, the card drawn (p. 94)
    is replaced and the deck is shuffled. What is the probability of obtaining a
    queen on the first draw and then a club on the second draw?
    (a) 1/52 × 1/52
    (b) 4/52 × 1/52
    (c) 4/52 × 9/52
    * (d) 4/52 × 13/52

31. A card is drawn from a standard deck. Before the next draw, the card drawn (p. 94)
    is replaced and the deck is shuffled. What is the probability of obtaining the
    ace of spades on the first draw and the two of clubs on the second draw?
    * (a) 1/52 × 1/52
    (b) 1/52 × 1/51
    (c) 4/52 × 4/52
    (d) 4/52 × 4/51

32. A card is drawn from a standard deck. Before the next draw, the card is (p. 94)
    thrown away (*not* replaced) and the deck is shuffled. What is the probability
    of obtaining the ace of spades on the first draw and the two of clubs on the
    second draw?
    (a) 1/52 × 1/52
    * (b) 1/52 × 1/51
    (c) 4/52 × 4/52
    (d) 4/52 × 4/51

33. A card is drawn from a standard deck. Before the next draw, the card is (p. 94)
    thrown away (*not* replaced) and the deck is shuffled. What is the probability
    of obtaining a king on the first draw and a ten on the second draw?
    (a) 1/52 × 1/52
    (b) 1/52 × 1/51
    (c) 4/52 × 4/52
    * (d) 4/52 × 4/51

34. You flip a coin seven times and obtain seven heads. You wish to determine (p. 95)
    the probability that the coin is fair. To carry out the necessary computations,
    you must:
    * (a) assume that the coin is fair.
    (b) assume that the coin is "loaded."
    (c) make no prior assumptions about the fairness of the coin.
    (d) flip the coin at least 100 times.

35. You flip a coin seven times and obtain seven heads. You want to decide (p. 95)
    whether the coin is fair. Which of the following computations and decisions
    is correct using the ".05 rule"?
    (a) 1/2 × 1/2 = .25, the coin is fair
    (b) 1/2 × 1/2 = .25, the coin is *not* fair
    (c) 1/2 × 1/2 × 1/2 × 1/2 × 1/2 × 1/2 × 1/2 = .008, the coin is fair
    * (d) 1/2 × 1/2 × 1/2 × 1/2 × 1/2 × 1/2 × 1/2 = .008, the coin is *not* fair

36. If the probability of obtaining six heads in six flips of a coin is (p. 95)
    approximately .02, and you therefore decide that the coin is "loaded"
    in favor of falling heads up, what is the probability that your decision is *incorrect*?
    (a) Zero—the coin must be "loaded" in favor of falling heads up
    * (b) 1/50—it is possible but very unlikely that the coin is fair
    (c) 1/2—your decision is likely to be wrong because seven flips is a very small number
    (d) Cannot be determined from the information given

37. You want to decide whether a coin is "loaded" in favor of falling heads up. (p. 95)
    You flip the coin three times and obtain three heads. What should you
    decide using the ".05 rule"?
    (a) The coin is fair.
    (b) The coin is "loaded" in favor of falling heads up.
    * (c) This experiment is poorly designed because you can never conclude that the coin
        is "loaded".
    (d) The next flip is likely to be a tail.

38. At the outset of an experiment, which of the following is assumed to (pp. 95–96)
    be true?
    * (a) Hypothesis 0
    (b) Hypothesis 1
    (c) *Both* of the above
    (d) *Neither* of the above

39. The probability of obtaining one head on one flip of a coin is equal to 1/2: (p. 95)
   * (a) only if Hypothesis 0 is true and the coin is fair.
   (b) only if Hypothesis 1 is true and the coin is "loaded".
   (c) always.
   (d) never.

40. To change the assumption that we make at the outset of an experiment, the results must be "sufficiently unlikely" to occur if that hypothesis is true. "Sufficiently unlikely" is most often defined as having a probability of: (p. 96)
   (a) .50 or less.
   (b) .10 or less.
   * (c) .05 or less.
   (d) .001 or less.

41. If we decide that the result of an experiment is "sufficiently unlikely" to occur if our initial hypothesis is true, and we therefore decide to reject the initial hypothesis using the ".05 rule", what is the probability that our decision is *incorrect*? (p. 96)
   (a) Zero—the decision must be correct because we used inferential statistics
   (b) 1/50
   * (c) 1/20
   (d) 1/5

42. A summary of the probability of all possible events of a specific type (for example, all possible results of flipping a coin six times) is called a(n): (p. 99)
   (a) binomial distribution.
   (b) outcome estimate.
   (c) probability table.
   * (d) statistical model.

Questions 43–49 refer to the table shown below:

Possible Results of
Flipping a Coin Six Times

Number of Heads	Probability
0	.016
1	.094
2	.234
3	.312
4	.234
5	.094
6	.016

43. All possible outcomes of flipping a coin six times are listed in this table. (p. 99)
    Therefore, the sum of the probability column must be:
    (a) 0
    (b) .5
    * (c) 1.0
    (d) 6.0

44. What is the probability of obtaining exactly four heads in six flips? (p. 99)
    (a) .344
    * (b) .234
    (c) .094
    (d) .016

45. What is the probability of obtaining *four or more* heads in six flips? (p. 99)
    * (a) .344
    (b) .234
    (c) .094
    (d) .016

46. Using the ".05 rule", what results must we obtain in order to decide that (p. 99)
    the coin is loaded?
    * (a) six heads or six tails
    (b) five or more heads
    (c) five or more heads *or* five or more tails
    (d) We can never decide that the coin is loaded

47. What is the probability of obtaining *either* six heads *or* six tails in six flips? (p. 99)
    (a) .016
    * (b) .032
    (c) .094
    (d) .11

48. What is the probability of obtaining *either* zero or one tail in six flips? (p. 99)
    (a) .016
    (b) .032
    (c) .094
    * (d) .11

49. If we flip the coin six times, what is the most likely result and how likely is this result? (p. 99)
    * (a) Three heads and three tails, probability = .312
    (b) Three heads and three tails, probability = .5
    (c) All possible results are equally likely, probability = .143
    (d) Cannot be determined from the information given

Questions 50–53 refer to the table shown below:

Possible Results of
Flipping a Coin Three Times

Number of Heads	Probability
0	.125
1	.375
2	.375
3	.125

50. All possible outcomes of flipping a coin three times are listed in this table. Therefore, the sum of the probability column must be: (p. 99)
    (a) 0
    (b) .5
    * (c) 1.0
    (d) 3.0

51. What is the probability of obtaining exactly two heads in three flips? (p. 99)
    (a) .5
    * (b) .375
    (c) .25
    (d) .125

52. What is the probability of obtaining *two or more* heads in three flips? (p. 99)
    * (a) .5
    (b) .375
    (c) .25
    (d) .125

53. Using the ".05 rule", we should decide that this coin is "loaded" in favor of falling heads up: (p .99)
    (a) only if we obtain three heads in three flips.
    (b) if we obtain two or three heads in three flips.
    (c) if we obtain one, two, or three heads in three flips.
    * (d) never—the experiment is poorly designed.

54. A *random sample* is one where: (p. 100)
    (a) each element in the population has an equal chance of being included in the sample.
    (b) all possible samples of the given size are equally likely to occur.
    * (c) *both* of the above
    (d) *neither* of the above

55. Suppose we draw 1,000 samples of size 100 from a large population and compute the mean of each sample. If we graph the distribution of 1,000 sample means, the shape will be: (p. 102)
    * (a) approximately normal.
    (b) negatively skewed.
    (c) positively skewed.
    (d) the same shape as the distribution of raw scores in the population.

56. In behavioral science research, which of the following serves the same purpose as the table listing all possible outcomes of six flips of a coin and the corresponding probabilities in the coin experiment? (p. 99)
    (a) A table that lists all favorable and unfavorable events
    (b) A parameter, such as the population mean
    (c) A statistic, such as the sample mean
    * (d) A statistical model, such as the normal curve

57. In behavioral science research: (p. 102)
    (a) the normal curve model is used in most situations.
    (b) the normal curve model is used only when the distribution of raw scores in the population is normal.
    * (c) different statistical models are used in different situations.
    (d) statistical models are rarely used.

58. Suppose we draw 1,000 samples of size 100 from a large population and compute the mean of each sample. The distribution of sample means is called a(n): (p. 100)
    * (a) experimental sampling distribution.
    (b) inferential sampling distribution.
    (c) statistical sampling distribution.
    (d) theoretical sampling distribution.

59. Suppose we draw 1,000 samples of size 100 from a large population (pp. 100, 102) and compute the mean of each sample. The resulting distribution of sample means:
    (a) serves as a statistical model for drawing inferences about the population mean.
    (b) is never used in practice because it would require too much effort to compute.
* (c) *both* of the above
    (d) *neither* of the above

60. In a large population, the distribution of raw scores is bimodal. If we draw (p. 102) 1,000 samples of size 100 and compute the mean of each sample, the distribution of sample means will be:
* (a) approximately normal and unimodal.
    (b) bimodal and symmetric.
    (c) bimodal and skewed to the left.
    (d) bimodal and skewed to the right.

Chapter 9

1. The normal curve is: (p. 105)
    (a) a bell-shaped, unimodal distribution.
    (b) a statistical model.
    (c) a theoretical sampling distribution.
    * (d) *all* of the above
    (e) *none* of the above

2. The normal curve is defined by: (p. 105)
    * (a) a mathematical formula that is never matched exactly by real data.
    (b) a large quantity of raw scores drawn from the same population.
    (c) a large quantity of sample means drawn from the same population.
    (d) a large quantity of standard deviations drawn from the same population.

3. If we wish to use the normal curve model to draw inferences about the *raw scores* in a population, what assumption must we make? (p. 105)
    (a) The distribution of raw scores in the sample is approximately normal.
    * (b) The distribution of raw scores in the population is approximately normal.
    (c) The distribution of sample means is approximately normal.
    (d) *None* of the above—no assumptions are necessary.

4. All bell-shaped, unimodal distributions are normal curves. (p. 108)
    (a) True
    * (b) False

5. When drawing inferences about the raw scores in a population, the total area under the normal curve: (p. 105)
    (a) increases as the size of the sample increases.
    (b) is equal to plus infinity.
    * (c) is defined as 100%.
    (d) has a numerical value equal to the number of cases in the population.

6. What problem do we resolve by using the normal curve model to draw inferences about the raw scores in a population? (p. 105)
    * (a) We obtain information about a population that is too large to measure.
    (b) We obtain more accurate results than we would get by measuring the entire population.
    (c) We don't have to make any assumptions about the raw scores in the population.
    (d) We can draw inferences about the samples we are studying.

7. Why is the normal curve table given in terms of z scores rather than raw scores? (pp. 106–107)
    (a) z scores are more accurate than raw scores.
    (b) All statistical tables are given in terms of z scores.
    * (c) Too many tables would be needed if raw scores were used.
    (d) To emphasize that we are using the normal curve model.

8. The entries in the normal curve table tell us: (p. 107)
    (a) The percent area between any two points under the normal curve.
    * (b) The percent area between the mean and the scores expressed as z scores.
    (c) The percent area between the mean and the raw scores.
    (d) The percent area between the median and the raw scores.

9. The normal curve table shows when you are working with a score below the mean by assigning a minus sign to the corresponding z score. (p. 107)
    (a) True
    * (b) False

10. In the normal curve, the area between the mean and a z score of +1.00 is _____ the area between a z score of +1.00 and a z score of +2.00. (p. 108)
    (a) smaller than
    (b) equal to
    * (c) greater than
    (d) cannot be determined from the information given

11. In the normal curve, which of the following areas contains the greatest number of cases? (p. 108)
    (a) Between $z = -2.00$ and $z = -1.50$
    * (b) Between $z = 0$ and $z = +.50$
    (c) Between $z = +1.00$ and $z = +1.50$
    (d) All of the above contain an equal number of cases.

12. If we draw one case at random from a population where the raw scores are normally distributed, which of the following is most likely to occur? (p. 108)
    * (a) A z score between 0 and –0.25
    (b) A z score between +1.00 and +1.25
    (c) A z score between +2.00 and +2.25
    (d) All of the above are equally likely.

13. A z score of −4.00 or less and a z score of +4.00 or more are so unlikely   (p. 109)
    as to suggest an error in computation.
    * (a) True
    (b) False

14. In the normal curve, the area between the mean and a z score of − 0.85 is   (p. 108)
    equal to the area between the mean and a z score of +0.85.
    * (a) True
    (b) False

Questions 15–29 refer to a population where the raw scores are normally distributed with a mean of 500 and a standard deviation of 100, and make use of the portion of the Normal Curve Table shown below.

Percent Area Under the Normal
Curve Between the Mean and z

z	Percent
0.25	9.87
0.50	19.15
0.52	19.85
0.75	27.34
0.84	29.95
1.00	34.13
1.25	39.44
1.28	39.97
1.50	43.32
1.65	45.05
1.75	45.99
2.00	47.72
2.33	49.01
2.58	49.51

15. What percentage of raw scores in the population can be expected to fall   (p. 109)
    between 500 and 625?
    (a) 10%
    (b) 27%
    * (c) 39%
    (d) 46%

16. What percentage of raw scores in the population can be expected to fall between 425 and 500? (p. 110)
    (a) 10%
    * (b) 27%
    (c) 39%
    (d) 46%

17. What percentage of the population can be expected to have raw scores between 325 and 575? (p. 111)
    (a) 37%
    (b) 43%
    (c) 55%
    * (d) 73%

18. What percentage of the population can be expected to have scores between 600 and 650? (p. 111)
    * (a) 9%
    (b) 19%
    (c) 43%
    (d) 77%

19. What percentage of the population can be expected to have scores above 665? (p. 112)
    (a) 1%
    * (b) 5%
    (c) 45%
    (d) 95%

20. What percentage of the population can be expected to have scores below 375? (p. 112)
    * (a) 11%
    (b) 19%
    (c) 27%
    (d) 39%

21. What is the probability that a person drawn at random from the population will have a score of 650 or more? (p. 113)
    (a) .05
    * (b) .07
    (c) .41
    (d) .43

22. What is the probability that a person drawn at random from the population will have a score of 300 or less? (p. 113)
    * (a) .02
    (b) .16
    (c) .34
    (d) .48

23. What raw score is needed for a person to be in the top 10% of the population? (p. 113)
    (a) 525
    (b) 600
    * (c) 628
    (d) 665

24. What raw score is needed for a person to be in the bottom 20% of the population? (p. 113)
    * (a) 416
    (b) 448
    (c) 552
    (d) 584

25. What raw score separates the top 70% of the population from the bottom 30%? (p. 114)
    (a) 416
    * (b) 448
    (c) 552
    (d) 584

26. What raw score separates the top 20% of the population from the bottom 80%? (p. 114)
    (a) 416
    (b) 448
    (c) 552
    * (d) 584

27. What raw score is needed to rank in the top 1% percent of the population? (p. 114)
    (a) 665
    (b) 700
    * (c) 733
    (d) 758

28. 99% of the raw scores in the population fall between what values? (p. 114)
    (a) 335 and 665
    (b) 300 and 700
    (c) 267 and 733
    * (d) 242 and 758

29. 95% of the raw scores in the population fall between what values? (p. 114)
    (a) 335 and 665
    * (b) 300 and 700
    (c) 267 and 733
    (d) 242 and 758

Questions 30–45 refer to a population where the raw scores are normally distributed with a mean of 34.0 and a standard deviation of 6.0, and make use of the portion of the Normal Curve Table shown below.

Percent Area Under the Normal
Curve Between the Mean and z

z	Percent
0.25	9.87
0.33	12.93
0.50	19.15
0.52	19.85
0.67	24.86
0.84	29.95
1.00	34.13
1.28	39.97
1.33	40.82
1.50	43.32
1.65	45.05
1.67	45.25
2.00	47.72
2.33	49.01
2.58	49.51

30. What percentage of raw scores in the population can be expected to fall between 34 and 38? (p. 109)
    (a) 12%
    (b) 19%
    * (c) 25%
    (d) 34%

31. What percentage of raw scores in the population can be expected to fall (p. 110)
    between 26 and 34?
    (a) 12%
    (b) 34%
    * (c) 41%
    (d) 43%

32. What percentage of the population can be expected to have raw scores (p. 111)
    between 30 and 42?
    (a) 16%
    (b) 37%
    (c) 41%
    * (d) 65%

33. What percentage the population can be expected to have raw scores (p. 111)
    between 37 and 46?
    (a) 19%
    (b) 29%
    (c) 48%
    * (d) 67%

34. What percentage of the population can be expected to have raw scores (p. 111)
    between 30 and 31?
    * (a) 6%
    (b) 19%
    (c) 25%
    (d) 44%

35. What percentage of the population can be expected to have scores (p. 112)
    above 43?
    * (a) 7%
    (b) 43%
    (c) 57%
    (d) 93%

36. What percentage of the population can be expected to have scores (p. 112)
    below 24?
    (a) 1%
    * (b) 5%
    (c) 45%
    (d) 95%

37. What is the probability that a person drawn at random from the population   (p. 113)
    will have a raw score of 40 or less?
    (a) .10
    (b) .16
    (c) .34
    * (d) .84

38. What is the probability that a person drawn at random from the population   (p. 113)
    will have a raw score of 43 or more?
    * (a) .07
    (b) .43
    (c) .45
    (d) .93

39. What is the probability that a person drawn at random from the population   (p. 113)
    will have a raw score of 31 or more?
    (a) .19
    (b) .31
    * (c) .69
    (d) .81

40. What is the probability that a person drawn at random from the population   (p. 113)
    will have a raw score of 26 or less?
    (a) .05
    (b) .09
    (c) .41
    (d) .45

41. What raw score is needed for a person to be in the top 1% of the   (p. 113)
    population?
    (a) 46
    (b) 47
    * (c) 48
    (d) 49

42. What raw score is needed for a person to be in the top 10% of the   (p. 113)
    population?
    (a) 35
    * (b) 42
    (c) 44
    (d) 48

43. What raw score separates the top 20% of the population from the bottom 80%? (p. 114)
    (a) 29
    (b) 31
    (c) 37
    * (d) 39

44. What raw score separates the top 90% of the population from the bottom 10%? (p. 114)
    * (a) 26
    (b) 32.5
    (c) 35.5
    (d) 42

45. 95% of the raw scores in the population fall between what values? (p. 114)
    * (a) 22 and 46
    (b) 24 and 44
    (c) 25 and 43
    (d) 26 and 42

Chapter 10

1. If we draw 1,000 samples of size 100 from a population and compute the (p. 118)
   mean of each sample, the distribution of sample means will be:
   * (a) approximately normal.
   (b) approximately normal only if the raw scores in the population are normally distributed.
   (c) negatively skewed.
   (d) positively skewed.

2. If we draw 1,000 samples of size 100 from a population and compute the (p. 118)
   mean of each sample, the *variability* of the distribution of sample means will be _____ the variability of the raw scores in each sample.
   * (a) smaller than
   (b) equal to
   (c) greater than
   (d) cannot be determined from the information given

3. If a sample of 25 people has a mean of 5.0 and a standard deviation of 2.5, (p. 119)
   the standard error of the mean is:
   (a) .1
   (b) .2
   * (c) .5
   (d) 1.0

4. If a sample of 100 people has a mean of 34 and a standard deviation of 7, (p. 119)
   the standard error of the mean is:
   (a) .07
   (b) .34
   * (c) .7
   (d) 3.4

5. If we draw two samples from the same population, one with 100 cases and (p. 119)
   one with 25 cases, for which sample will the standard error of the mean be *smaller*?
   (a) The sample with 25 cases
   * (b) The sample with 100 cases
   (c) The standard error of the mean will be the same for both samples because they come from the same population.
   (d) Cannot be determined from the information given

6. A researcher wishes to estimate the mean of a population as accurately as (p. 119)
possible. The researcher wants the standard error of the mean to be:
   * (a) small.
   (b) medium.
   (c) large.
   (d) equal to the sample size.

7. The standard error of the mean tells us: (p.119)
   (a) the variability of means of samples of the same size drawn from the same population.
   (b) how trustworthy a single sample mean is as an estimate of the corresponding population mean.
   * (c) *both* of the above
   (d) *neither* of the above

8. If we were able to measure the entire population, the standard error of the (p. 119)
mean would be:
   * (a) zero.
   (b) 1.0.
   (c) plus infinity.
   (d) equal to the standard deviation of the raw scores.

9. What are the smallest and largest possible values of the standard error (p. 119)
of the mean?
   (a) Minus infinity and plus infinity
   (b) −1.00 and +1.00
   (c) 0 and plus infinity
   * (d) 0 and the standard deviation of the raw scores

10. As the size of the sample increases, the standard error of the mean: (p. 119)
   * (a) becomes smaller.
   (b) remains the same.
   (c) becomes larger.
   (d) cannot be determined from the information given

11. In hypothesis testing, which of the following is assumed to be true at the (p. 122)
beginning of the research study?
   (a) The alternative hypothesis
   * (b) The null hypothesis
   (c) *Both* of the above
   (d) *Neither* of the above

12. In a *two-tailed* test about the mean of one population, the *null hypothesis* (p. 122)
    specifies:
    (a) a single value of the sample mean.
    (b) a range of values of the sample mean.
    * (c) a single value of the population mean.
    (d) a range of values of the population mean.

13. In a *one-tailed* test about the mean of one population, the *null hypothesis* (p. 139)
    specifies:
    (a) a single value of the sample mean.
    (b) a range of values of the sample mean.
    (c) a single value of the population mean.
    * (d) a range of values of the population mean.

14. When testing a hypothesis about the mean of one population, *sampling* (p. 121)
    error occurs when:
    (a) the cases that happen to be included in the sample are *not* typical of the population.
    (b) the sample mean is different from the population mean.
    * (c) *both* of the above
    (d) *neither* of the above

15. When testing a hypothesis about the mean of one population, the only (p. 119)
    way to avoid sampling error is to:
    (a) use the standard error of the mean.
    (b) use a random sample.
    (c) draw a large number of samples of size 100.
    * (d) measure the entire population.

16. A *Type I error* occurs when the researcher: (p. 123)
    (a) rejects a false null hypothesis.
    * (b) rejects a true null hypothesis.
    (c) retains a false null hypothesis
    (d) retains a true null hypothesis.

17. A *Type II error* occurs when the researcher: (p. 123)
    (a) rejects a false null hypothesis.
    (b) rejects a true null hypothesis.
    * (c) retains a false null hypothesis.
    (d) retains a true null hypothesis.

18. Using the .05 criterion of significance, the probability of making a (p. 123)
    Type I error is:
    * (a) .05.
    (b) .95.
    (c) equal to the standard error of the mean.
    (d) cannot be determined from the information given

19. Using the .05 criterion of significance, the probability of making a (p. 123)
    Type II error is:
    (a) .05.
    (b) .95.
    (c) equal to the standard error of the mean.
    (d) cannot be determined from the information given

20. Using the .01 criterion of significance, the probability of making a (p. 123)
    Type I error is equal to:
    (a) .01.
    (b) .99.
    (c) the standard error of the mean.
    (d) cannot be determined from the information given

21. Using the .01 criterion of significance, the probability of making a (p. 123)
    Type II error is equal to:
    (a) .01.
    (b) .99.
    (c) the standard error of the mean.
    * (d) cannot be determined from the information given

22. Which of the following criteria of significance is most likely to lead to a (p. 124)
    Type I error?
    * (a) .10
    (b) .05
    (c) .01
    (d) .001

23. Which of the following criteria of significance is most likely to lead to a (p. 124)
    Type II error?
    (a) .10
    (b) .05
    (c) .01
    * (d) .001

24. If we switch from the .05 criterion of significance to the .01 criterion of significance: (p. 124)
    (a) a Type I error becomes more likely and a Type II error becomes less likely.
    * (b) a Type I error becomes less likely and a Type II error becomes more likely.
    (c) both a Type I error and a Type II error become less likely.
    (d) the probability of a Type I error and a Type II error remains the same.

25. Why do researchers usually *not* use the .001 criterion of significance? (p. 124)
    (a) It would make a Type I error too likely.
    * (b) It would make a Type II error too likely.
    (c) It would make *both* a Type I error and a Type II error too likely.

26. Why do researchers usually *not* use the .10 criterion of significance? (p. 124)
    * (a) It would make a Type I error too likely.
    (b) It would make a Type II error too likely.
    (c) It would make *both* a Type I error and a Type II error too likely.

27. The theory or idea that the researcher hopes to support is usually specified by the: (p. 124)
    * (a) alternative hypothesis.
    (b) criterion of significance.
    (c) null hypothesis.
    (d) none of the above

28. What are the practical consequences of a *Type I error*? (p. 124)
    * (a) A false positive—erroneously concluding that the researcher's theory has been supported
    (b) A false negative—erroneously concluding that the researcher's theory was *not* supported
    (c) Either a false positive or a false negative, depending on the direction (sign) of the results

29. What are the practical consequences of a *Type II error*? (p. 124)
    (a) A false positive—erroneously concluding that the researcher's theory has been supported
    * (b) A false negative—erroneously concluding that the researcher's theory was *not* supported
    (c) Either a false positive or a false negative, depending on the direction (sign) of the results

30. If the sample size is very small, which of the following is *more likely?* (pp. 119, 128)
    (a) A false positive—erroneously concluding that the researcher's theory has been supported
    * (b) A false negative—erroneously concluding that the researcher's theory was *not* supported
    (c) Both of the above are equally likely
    (d) Neither of the above—sample size has no effect on the likelihood of a false positive or a false negative

31. The *power* of a statistical test is equal to the probability of: (p. 123)
    (a) retaining the null hypothesis when it is true.
    (b) rejecting the null hypothesis when it is true.
    (c) retaining the null hypothesis when it is false.
    * (d) rejecting the null hypothesis when it is false.

32. A statistical test that has *low power:* (p. 123)
    (a) occurs when the sample size is very large.
    (b) is less likely to lead to a Type I error.
    (c) is less likely to lead to a Type II Error.
    * (d) is likely to be a waste of time and effort.

33. If the results of a statistical test indicate that we should *retain* the null hypothesis, the correct way to state the conclusion is: (p. 128)
    (a) we accept the null hypothesis as true.
    * (b) there is not sufficient reason to reject the null hypothesis.
    (c) the experimenter's theory is wrong.
    (d) *all* of the above
    (e) *none* of the above

34. When drawing inferences about the mean of one population, the correct statistical model to use is: (pp. 127, 129)
    (a) the normal curve.
    (b) the t distributions.
    (c) the t distributions if the population standard deviation is known and the normal curve if the population standard deviation is *not* known.
    * (d) the normal curve if the population standard deviation is known and the t distributions if the population standard deviation is *not* known.

35. A sample of N = 100 has a mean of 42.9. The population standard deviation (p. 128)
    is known to be 7.5. Which of the following null-hypothesized values of the
    population mean should be *rejected* using the .05 criterion of significance?
    * (a) 41.1
    (b) 42.1
    (c) 44.1
    (d) *All* of the above
    (e) *None* of the above

36. A sample of N = 100 has a mean of 34.7. The population standard deviation (p. 128)
    is known to be 6.0. Which of the following null-hypothesized values of the
    population mean should be *rejected* using the .05 criterion of significance?
    (a) 33.8
    (b) 35.0
    (c) 35.5
    (d) *All* of the above
    * (e) *None* of the above

37. If we test the null hypothesis that the mean of a population is 84.2, and the (p. 133)
    results of a two-tailed test indicate that the null hypothesis should be rejected
    using the .05 criterion significance, the correct conclusion is:
    * (a) the population mean is not exactly equal to 84.2.
    (b) the population mean is at least 2 points above or below 84.2.
    (c) the population mean is at least 5 points above or below 84.2.
    (d) it is likely that the population mean is 84.2.

Questions 38–43 refer to the study described below:

A researcher wishes to test the hypothesis that the mean IQ at a particular university is
different from the average of 100. The researcher obtains a sample of 100 students. The
mean of this sample is 103.6 and the standard deviation is 15.0.

38. The *null hypothesis* states that the population mean is: (p. 122)
    * (a) equal to 100.
    (b) *not* equal to 100.
    (c) less than 100.
    (d) greater than 100.

39. The *alternative hypothesis* states that the population mean is: (p. 122)
    (a) equal to 100.
    * (b) *not* equal to 100.
    (c) greater than 100.
    (d) less than 100.

40. If the statistical analysis indicates that the null hypothesis should be (p. 128)
    retained, the researcher should conclude that the population mean is:
    (a) equal to 100.0.
    (b) not exactly equal to 100.0.
    (c) less than 100.0.
    (d) greater than 100.0.
    * (e) none of the above

41. If the statistical analysis indicates that the null hypothesis should be (p. 128)
    rejected, the researcher should conclude that the population mean is:
    (a) equal to 100.0.
    * (b) not exactly equal to 100.0.
    (c) 102 or higher.
    (d) at least 5 points above or below 100.0.
    (e) none of the above

42. Using the .05 criterion or significance, the critical value of t is 1.99.   (pp. 131, 123)
    What should the researcher decide, and what error might the researcher make?
    (a) Retain the null hypothesis—Type I error.
    (b) Retain the null hypothesis—Type II error.
    * (c) Reject the null hypothesis—Type I error.
    (d) Reject the null hypothesis—Type II error.

43. Using the .01 criterion of significance, the critical value of t is 2.64.   (pp. 131, 123)
    What should the researcher decide, and what error might the researcher make?
    (a) Retain the null hypothesis—Type I error.
    * (b) Retain the null hypothesis—Type II error.
    (c) Reject the null hypothesis—Type I error.
    (d) Reject the null hypothesis—Type II error.

44. If we specify a range of values within which a parameter (such as a (p. 133)
    population mean) is likely to fall, this range is called:
    * (a) a confidence interval.
    (b) confidence limits.
    (c) a point estimate.
    (d) a statistical estimate.

45. If we switch from the 95% confidence interval to the 99% confidence interval: (p. 135)
    * (a) we can be more sure that the population mean falls within the confidence interval.
    (b) we will estimate the population mean more precisely.
    (c) both of the above
    (d) neither of the above

46. When drawing inferences about the mean of one population, the 95% (p. 135)
    confidence interval specifies all of the null-hypothesized values of the
    population mean that should be:
    (a) rejected using the .05 criterion of significance.
    * (b) retained using the .05 criterion of significance.
    (c) rejected using the .01 criterion of significance.
    (d) retained using the .01 criterion of significance.

47. The 95% confidence interval for the mean of a population is 23.4 to 38.6. (p. 134)
    Using hypothesis testing and the .05 criterion of significance, which of the
    following null hypotheses should be *retained*?
    (a) Population mean = 25.7
    (b) Population mean = 34.2
    (c) Population mean = 38.1
    * (d) *All* of the above
    (e) *None* of the above

48. The 95% confidence interval for the mean of a population is 87.5 to 113.4. (p. 134)
    Using hypothesis testing and the .05 criterion of significance, which of the
    following null hypotheses should be *rejected*?
    (a) Population mean = 90.2
    (b) Population mean = 105.7
    * (c) Population mean = 115.6
    (d) *All* of the above
    (e) *None* of the above

49. The 95% confidence interval for the mean of a population is from 25.8 to 40.1. (p. 135)
    Which of the following *cannot* be the 99% confidence interval for the same
    population mean?
    (a) 20.6 to 45.3
    * (b) 27.0 to 38.9
    (c) *Both* of the above
    (d) *Neither* of the above

50. The 99% confidence interval for the mean of a population is 102.7 to 120.4. (p. 135)
    Which of the following *cannot* be the 95% confidence interval for the same
    population mean?
    (a) 100.3 to 122.8
    (b) 98.6 to 124.5
    * (c) *Both* of the above
    (d) *Neither* of the above

Questions 51–58 refer to the research study described below:

A researcher theorizes that students at a particular university differ in intelligence from the average IQ of 100. The researcher computes the 95% confidence interval for the mean of this population. Four possible results are shown below:

>   Result 1:   91.6–109.4
>   Result 2:   99.1–116.9
>   Result 3:   101.2–119.0
>   Result 4:   112.7–130.5

51. For which result(s) should the researcher *retain* the null hypothesis that (p. 134)
    the population mean is equal to 100.0?
    (a) Only result 1
    * (b) Results 1 and 2
    (c) Results 3 and 4
    (d) Only result 4

52. For which result(s) should the researcher *reject* the null hypothesis that (p. 134)
    the population mean is equal to 100.0?
    (a) Only result 1
    (b) Results 1 and 2
    * (c) Results 3 and 4
    (d) Only result 4

53. Which result most strongly *contradicts* the researcher's theory? (p. 135)
    * (a) Result 1
    (b) Result 2
    (c) *Both* result 1 and result 2 provide equally strong evidence against the researcher's theory.
    (d) *Neither* result 1 nor result 2 provides any evidence against the researcher's theory.

54. Which result most strongly *supports* the researcher's theory? (p. 135)
    (a) Result 3
    * (b) Result 4
    (c) *Both* result 3 and result 4 provide equally strong support for the researcher's theory.
    (d) *Neither* result 3 nor result 4 supports the researcher's theory.

55. Which result indicates that the mean IQ at this university is likely to be (p. 134)
    at least 112?
    (a) Result 1
    (b) Result 2
    (c) Result 3
    * (d) Result 4

56. Which result indicates that the mean IQ at this university, while probably (p. 134)
    greater than 100, is likely to be as low as 102?
    (a) Result 1
    (b) Result 2
    * (c) Result 3
    (d) Result 4

57. Which result indicates that the mean IQ at this university is likely to be (p. 134)
    100 and as low as 92?
    * (a) Result 1
    (b) Result 2
    (c) Result 3
    (d) Result 4

58. Which result indicates that the mean IQ at this university is likely to be 100 (p. 134)
    but is *not* likely to be less than 99?
    (a) Result 1
    * (b) Result 2
    (c) Result 3
    (d) Result 4

59. When drawing inferences about the *proportion* of one population, (p. 136)
    the correct statistical model to use is:
    * (a) the normal curve.
    (b) the t distributions.
    (c) the t distributions if the population standard deviation is known and the normal curve if the population standard deviation is *not* known.
    (d) the normal curve if the population standard deviation is known and the t distributions if the population standard deviation is *not* known.

60. The standard error of a proportion tells us: (p. 136)
    (a) the variability of proportions obtained from samples of the same size drawn from the same population.
    (b) how trustworthy a single sample proportion is as an estimate of the corresponding population proportion.
  * (c) *both* of the above
    (d) *neither* of the above

61. A researcher wants to estimate the proportion of a population as accurately (p. 136) as possible. The researcher wants the standard error of the proportion to be:
  * (a) small.
    (b) medium.
    (c) large.
    (d) equal to the sample size.

62. As the size of the sample increases, the standard error of the proportion: (p. 136)
  * (a) becomes smaller.
    (b) remains the same.
    (c) becomes larger.
    (d) cannot be determined from the information given

63. A few weeks before an election, a politician takes a poll and finds that 55% (p. 136) of the sample intends to vote for her, while 45% intends to vote for her opponent. If the standard error of a proportion is .5, what should the politician conclude?
    (a) She is likely to win the election.
  * (b) The election is too close to call.
    (c) She is likely to lose the election.
    (d) Cannot be determined from the information given

Questions 64–69 refer to the research study described below:

A researcher predicts that the mean IQ of a specified population is *greater than* 100. She therefore decides to use a one-tailed test. She also selects the .05 criterion of significance. Four possible results, expressed as 95% confidence intervals, are shown below:

       Result 1:   84.2 – 91.6
       Result 2:   95.3 – 102.7
       Result 3:   100.7 – 108.1
       Result 4:   108.8 – 116.2

64. Using hypothesis testing, the *null hypothesis* states that the population mean is: (p. 139)
    (a) equal to 100.0.
    (b) *not* equal to 100.0.
    * (c) less than or equal to 100.0.
    (d) greater than or equal to 100.0.

65. Using hypothesis testing, the alternative hypothesis states that the population mean is: (p. 139)
    (a) equal to 100.0.
    (b) *not* equal to 100.0.
    (c) less than 100.0.
    * (d) greater than 100.0.

66. For which result(s) should the researcher *retain* the null hypothesis? (p. 141)
    (a) Result 1
    (b) Result 2
    * (c) *Both* result 1 and result 2
    (d) Neither result 1 nor result 2

67. For which result(s) should the researcher *reject* the null hypothesis? (p. 141)
    (a) Result 3
    (b) Result 4
    * (c) *Both* result 3 and result 4
    (d) *Neither* result 3 nor result 4

68. Which result most strongly supports the researcher's theory? (p. 141)
    (a) Result 1
    (b) Result 2
    (c) Result 3
    * (d) Result 4

69. For which result should the experimenter repeat the study with a new sample of subjects and a two-tailed test? (p. 141)
    * (a) Result 1
    (b) Result 2
    (c) Result 3
    (d) Result 4
    (e) *None* of the above

Chapter 11

1. When drawing inferences about the difference between the means (p. 153)
   of two populations, the correct statistical model to use is:
   (a) the normal curve.
   * (b) the t distributions.
   (c) chi square.
   (d) *none* of the above

2. The standard error of the difference shows how trustworthy a single (p. 148)
   difference between two sample means is as an estimate of the difference
   between the corresponding population means.
   * (a) True
   (b) False

3. A researcher wants to estimate the difference between two population (p. 148)
   means as accurately as possible. The researcher wants the standard error
   of the difference to be:
   * (a) small.
   (b) medium.
   (c) large.
   (d) equal to the sample size.

4. As the size of the sample increases, the standard error of the difference: (p. 151)
   * (a) becomes smaller.
   (b) remains the same.
   (c) becomes larger.
   (d) cannot be determined from the information given

5. If we were able to measure the entire population, the standard error of (p. 151)
   the difference would be:
   * (a) zero.
   (b) 1.0.
   (c) equal to the pooled variance.
   (d) equal to the standard deviation of the raw scores.

6. We draw two samples of N = 100 from two different populations and compute the difference between the sample means. We then do the same using samples of N = 25. In which case will the standard error of the difference be *smaller*? (p. 151)
   (a) Using a sample size of 25
   * (b) Using a sample size of 100
   (c) The standard error of the difference will be the same in both cases.
   (d) Cannot be determined from the information given

7. The t test for two independent samples can be used to test the null hypothesis that the difference between two population means is any value, such as zero, 5, 20, or 138. (p. 152)
   * (a) True
   (b) False

Questions 8–15 refer to the research study described below:

A researcher wishes to test the theory that men and women differ on a measure of personality. The researcher draws a sample of 35 men and a sample of 35 women. The sample means on the personality measure are: men, 46.7; women, 51.4.

8. Why can't the researcher conclude, just by looking at the difference of 4.7 between the two sample means, that the difference between the population means is *not* zero? (p. 147)
   (a) The standard deviation of each sample has not been considered.
   (b) A sample size of 35 is too small to draw conclusions.
   * (c) Sampling error may have caused one or both samples to be unrepresentative of the corresponding population.
   (d) *None* of the above—the researcher should conclude that the difference between the population means is not zero.

9. The null hypothesis states that: (p. 152)
   (a) the means of the two samples are equal.
   * (b) the means of the two populations are equal.
   (c) the means of the two samples are *not* equal.
   (d) the means of the two populations are *not* equal.

10. If the statistical analysis indicates that the null hypothesis should be (pp. 155–156)
    retained, the researcher should conclude that:
    (a) men and women are the same on this personality measure.
    (b) men and women are *not* the same on this personality measure.
    (c) the difference between men and women on this personality measure is 4.7 or more.
    * (d) *none* of the above

11. If the statistical analysis indicates that the null hypothesis should be (p. 153)
    rejected, the researcher should conclude that:
    (a) men and women are the same on this personality measures.
    * (b) men and women are *not* the same on this personality measure.
    (c) the difference between men and women on this personality measure is 4.7 or more.
    (d) *none* of the above

12. Using the .05 criterion of significance, the critical value needed to reject (p. 156)
    the null hypothesis is 2.03. If the standard error of the difference is 2.0, what
    should the researcher decide and what error might be made?
    (a) Retain the null hypothesis—Type I error.
    (b) Retain the null hypothesis—Type II error.
    * (c) Reject the null hypothesis—Type I error.
    (d) Reject the null hypothesis—Type II error.

13. Using the .05 criterion of significance, the critical value needed to reject (p. 156)
    the null hypothesis is 2.03. If the standard error of the difference is 4.0,
    what should the researcher decide and what error might be made?
    (a) Retain the null hypothesis—Type I error.
    * (b) Retain the null hypothesis—Type II error.
    (c) Reject the null hypothesis—Type I error.
    (d) Reject the null hypothesis—Type II error.

14. If the statistical analysis indicates that the null hypothesis should be (p. 156)
    retained, the correct way to state the conclusion is:
    (a) the researcher's theory is correct.
    (b) the researcher's theory is incorrect.
    (c) there is no difference between the two population means.
    * (d) there is not sufficient reason to reject the hypothesis that the difference between the population means is zero.

15. If the statistical analysis indicates that the null hypothesis should be *rejected*, (p. 154)
    the correct way to state the conclusion is:
    * (a) the difference between the two population means is not exactly equal to zero.
    (b) the two population means differ by at least 2 or 3 points.
    (c) the two population means differ by at least the observed difference between the sample means.
    (d) there is a strong relationship between gender and scores on the personality measure.

16. When estimating the standard error of the difference, the *pooled* (pp. 151–152)
    variance:
    (a) gives greater weight to the larger of the two samples.
    (b) includes information about the variability of both samples.
    (c) serves the same purpose as s divided by the square root of N when estimating the standard error of the mean.
    * (d) *all* of the above

17. A researcher wishes to test the hypothesis that the difference between two (p. 152)
    population means is zero. If the sample means are 106.4 and 99.2, the standard error of the difference is 6.1, and the critical value needed to reject the null hypothesis is 2.09, what should the researcher decide about the difference between the two population means?
    (a) It is equal to 0.0.
    (b) It is *not* equal to 0.0.
    (c) It is at least 7.2.
    * (d) *None* of the above

18. A researcher wishes to test the hypothesis that the difference between two (p. 152)
    population means is zero. If the sample means are 106.4 and 99.2, the standard error of the difference is 2.3, and the critical value needed to reject the null hypothesis is 2.09, what should the researcher decide about the difference between the two population means?
    (a) It is equal to 0.
    * (b) It is *not* equal to 0.
    (c) It is at least 7.2.
    (d) *None* of the above

19. A researcher who obtains a statistically significant result for the difference   (p. 154)
    between two means should conclude that:
    (a) the result has practical importance.
    (b) there is a strong relationship between membership in a population and scores on the variable being studied.
    * (c) the result should be converted to a measure that shows strength of relationship.
    (d) the researcher's theory has been contradicted.

Questions 20–27 refer to the research study described below:

A researcher wishes to test the theory that men and women differ on a measure of personality. The researcher obtains samples of 50 men and 50 women and computes the 95% confidence interval for the difference between two means. Four possible results are shown below:

   Result 1: 10.0 to 19.7
   Result 2: 0.5 to 10.2
   Result 3: −0.4 to 9.3
   Result 4: −4.6 to 5.0

20. For which result(s) should the researcher *retain* the null hypothesis   (pp. 154–155)
    that the difference between the two population means is zero?
    (a) Only result 1
    (b) Results 1 and 2
    * (c) Results 3 and 4
    (d) Only result 4

21. For which result(s) should the researcher *reject* the null hypothesis   (pp. 154–155)
    that the difference between the two population means is zero?
    (a) only result 1
    * (b) Results 1 and 2
    (c) Results 3 and 4
    (d) Only result 4

22. Which result most strongly *supports* the researcher's theory?   (p. 155)
    * (a) Result 1
    (b) Result 2
    (c) *Both* results 1 and 2 provide equally strong support for the researcher's theory.
    (d) *Neither* result 1 nor result 2 supports the researcher's theory.

23. Which result most strongly *contradicts* the researcher's theory? (p. 155)
    (a) Result 3
    * (b) Result 4
    (c) *Both* results 3 and 4 provide equally strong evidence against the researcher's theory.
    (d) *Neither* result 3 nor result 4 contradicts the researcher's theory.

24. Which result indicates that the difference between the two population means is probably not zero but is likely to be as small as 1? (p. 155)
    (a) Result 1
    * (b) Result 2
    (c) Result 3
    (d) Result 4

25. Which result indicates that the difference between the two population means is probably not zero and is likely to be at least 10? (p. 155)
    * (a) Result 1
    (b) Result 2
    (c) Result 3
    (d) Result 4

26. Which result indicates that the difference between the two population means is likely to be zero and unlikely to be greater than 5? (p. 155)
    (a) Result 1
    (b) Result 2
    (c) Result 3
    * (d) Result 4

27. Which result indicates that the difference between the two population means is likely to be zero and is likely to be as large as 9? (p. 155)
    (a) Result 1
    (b) Result 2
    * (c) Result 3
    (d) Result 4

Questions 28–35 refer to the research study described below:

A researcher wishes to test the theory that students at two universities differ on a measure of intelligence that has a mean of 100 and a standard deviation of 15. The researcher obtains two samples of 50 students from each university and computes the 95% confidence interval for the difference between two means. Four possible results are shown below:

            Result   1:   −11.2 to   1.3
            Result   2:   −6.7 to   4.8
            Result   3:   1.2 to   9.6
            Result   4:   20.0 to 30.7

28. For which result(s) should the researcher *retain* the null hypothesis   (pp. 154–155)
    that the difference between the two population means is zero?
    (a) Only result 1
    * (b) Results 1 and 2
    (c) Results 3 and 4
    (d) Only result 4

29. For which result(s) should the researcher *reject* the null hypothesis   (pp. 154–155)
    that the difference between the two population means is zero?
    (a) Only result 1
    (b) Results 1 and 2
    * (c) Results 3 and 4
    (d) Only result 4

30. Which result most strongly *supports* the researcher's theory?   (p. 155)
    (a) Result 3
    * (b) Result 4
    (c) *Both* results 3 and 4 provide equally strong support for the researcher's theory.
    (d) *Neither* result 3 nor result 4 supports the researcher's theory.

31. Which result most strongly *contradicts* the researcher's theory?   (p. 155)
    (a) Result 1
    * (b) Result 2
    (c) *Both* results 1 and 2 provide equally strong evidence against the researcher's theory.
    (d) *Neither* result 1 nor result 2 contradicts the researcher's theory.

32. Which result indicates that the difference between the two population means is probably not zero but is likely to be as small as 2? (p. 155)
    (a) Result 1
    (b) Result 2
    * (c) Result 3
    (d) Result 4

33. Which result indicates that the difference between the two population means is likely to be zero and likely to be as large as 11? (p. 155)
    * (a) Result 1
    (b) Result 2
    (c) Result 3
    (d) Result 4

34. Which result indicates that the difference between the two population means is likely to be zero but unlikely to be larger than 7? (p. 155)
    (a) Result 1
    * (b) Result 2
    (c) Result 3
    (d) Result 4

35. Which result indicates that the difference between the two population means is probably not zero and likely to be at least 20? (p. 155)
    (a) Result 1
    (b) Result 2
    (c) Result 3
    * (d) Result 4

36. The 95% confidence interval for the difference between two means is −3.7 to 8.5. Which of the following *cannot* be the 99% confidence interval for the difference between the same two means? (pp. 154–155)
    * (a) −3.2 to 7.9
    (b) −5.6 to 11.2
    (c) *Both* of the above
    (d) *Neither* of the above

37. The 99% confidence interval for the difference between two means is −2.7 to 11.4. Which of the following *cannot* be the 95% confidence interval for the difference between the same two means? (pp. 154–155)
    (a) −3.2 to 12.1
    (b) −7.6 to 18.9
    * (c) *Both* of the above
    (d) *Neither* of the above

38. If we want to be *most sure* that the difference between two means falls within a confidence interval, which interval should we use? (p. 155)
    (a) The 95% confidence interval
    * (b) The 99% confidence interval
    (c) *Both* of the above allow us to be equally sure.

39. If we want to specify the difference between two means *most precisely*, which confidence interval should we use? (p. 155)
    * (a) The 95% confidence interval
    (b) The 99% confidence interval
    (c) *Both* of the above are equally precise.

40. When testing hypotheses about the difference between the means of two populations, the *degrees of freedom* are: (p. 152)
    (a) $N_1 + N_2$
    (b) $N_1 - N_2$
    (c) $N_1 + N_2 - 1$
    * (d) $N_1 + N_2 - 2$

41. If we *reject* the null hypothesis about the difference between two population means using the .05 criterion of significance, what is the probability that we have made a Type I error? (p. 156)
    (a) 0
    * (b) .05
    (c) .95
    (d) Cannot be determined from the information given

42. If we *retain* the null hypothesis about the difference between two population means using the .05 criterion of significance, what is the probability that we have made a Type II error? (p. 156)
    (a) 0
    (b) .05
    (c) .95
    * (d) Cannot be determined from the information given

43. If we *reject* the null hypothesis about the difference between two population means using the .05 criterion of significance, what is the probability that we have made a Type II error? (p. 156)
    * (a) 0
    (b) .05
    (c) .95
    (d) Cannot be determined from the information given

44. If we *retain* the null hypothesis about the difference between two population   (p. 156)
    means using the .05 criterion of significance, what is the probability that we
    have made a Type I error?
    * (a) 0
    (b) .05
    (c) .95
    (d) Cannot be determined from the information given

45. If we are testing a hypothesis about the difference between two population   (p. 156)
    means and we switch from the .05 criterion of significance to the .01
    criterion, what happens to the probabilities of a Type I error and a Type II error?
    (a) Both probabilities become smaller.
    * (b) The probability of a Type I error becomes smaller and the probability of a Type II
       error becomes larger.
    (c) The probability of a Type I error becomes larger and he probability of a Type II
       error becomes smaller.
    (d) Both probabilities become larger.

46. When using the t test for the difference between the means of two   (p. 156)
    populations:
    (a) the results will be accurate only if the variable is normally distributed within each
       population.
    * (b) if the variances of the two populations differ substantially, equal sample sizes
       should be used.
    (c) *both* of the above
    (d) *neither* of the above

47. A researcher wishes to test the hypothesis that a persuasive message about   (p. 157)
    our government will change people's attitudes toward politicians. Each subject's
    attitude is measured before and after receiving the message. The correct
    procedure to use is:
    (a) the t test with independent samples.
    (b) the z test with independent samples.
    * (c) the t test with matched samples.
    (d) the z test with matched samples.

48. When subjects can be matched, the matched t test is preferable to the t test   (p. 160)
    with independent samples because it is:
    * (a) more likely to reject a false null hypothesis.
    (b) more likely to reject a true null hypothesis.
    (c) more likely to retain the null hypothesis.
    (d) less time-consuming.

49. The mean of 15 subjects on an attitude scale after receiving a persuasive (p. 159)
    message is 38.4. The mean for the same subjects before receiving the
    message was 32.6. If the standard error of the mean of the differences is 9.7
    and the critical value needed to reject the null hypothesis is 2.145, the researcher
    should conclude that:
    (a) the message does *not* change people's attitudes.
    (b) the message changes people's attitudes.
    (c) the message changes people's attitudes by at least 5.8 points.
    * (d) *none* of the above

50. The mean of 100 subjects on an attitude scale after receiving a persuasive (p. 159)
    message is 38.4. The mean for the same subjects before receiving the
    message was 32.6. If the standard error of the mean of the differences is
    1.5 and the critical value needed to reject the null hypothesis is 1.99,
    the researcher should conclude that:
    (a) the message does *not* change people's attitudes.
    * (b) the message changes people's attitudes.
    (c) the message changes people's attitudes by at least 5.8 points.
    (d) *none* of the above

51. If a matched t test is carried out and the 95% confidence interval is (p. 160)
    computed, for which of the following intervals should the researcher
    retain the null hypothesis of zero change?
    (a) 1.06 to 7.79
    (b) 10.23 to 16.48
    (c) *Both* of the above
    * (d) *Neither* of the above

52. If a matched t test is carried out and the 95% confidence interval is (p. 160)
    computed, for which of the following intervals should the researcher
    reject the null hypothesis of zero change?
    (a) 1.06 to 7.79
    (b) 10.23 to 16.48
    * (c) *Both* of the above
    (d) *Neither* of the above

53. If a matched t test is carried out and the 95% confidence interval is (p. 160)
    computed, which of the following intervals most strongly supports
    the researcher's theory that the subjects will change?
    (a) 1.06 to 7.79
    * (b) 10.23 to 16.48
    (c) *Both* of the above provide equally strong evidence.
    (d) *Neither* of the above provides evidence of change.

54. For the matched t test, the *degrees of freedom* are: (p. 159)
    (a) the number of scores.
    (b) the number of pairs.
    (c) the number of scores minus 1.
    * (d) the number of pairs minus 1.

55. For the matched t test, the standard error term is equivalent to: (p. 157)
    * (a) the standard error of the mean.
    (b) the standard error of the difference.
    (c) the pooled variance.
    (d) *none* of the above

Chapter 12

1. Which of the following are positively correlated? (p. 164)
    - (a) Scores on a final exam and grades in that course
    - (b) Scores on a midterm exam and a final exam in the same course
    - * (c) *Both* of the above
    - (d) *Neither* of the above

2. Which of the following are positively correlated? (p. 164)
    - (a) Amount of time spent in studying and grades
    - (b) Annual income and amount of federal income tax owed
    - * (c) *Both* of the above
    - (d) *Neither* of the above

3. Which of the following are negatively correlated? (p. 165)
    - (a) Intelligence and height
    - * (b) Number of years playing golf and golf score
    - (c) *Both* of the above
    - (d) *Neither* of the above

4. Which of the following are uncorrelated? (p. 166)
    - * (a) Intelligence and height
    - (b) Number of years playing golf and golf score
    - (c) *Both* of the above
    - (d) *Neither* of the above

5. If two variables are highly positively correlated, which of the following must have approximately the same numerical value and the same sign? (p. 168)
    - (a) The paired raw scores
    - * (b) The paired Z scones
    - (c) *Both* of the above
    - (d) *Neither* of the above

6. If the sum of the paired differences between the Z scores on X and the Z scores on Y is close to zero, the correlation between X and Y is: (p. 170)
    - (a) approximately zero.
    - * (b) large and positive.
    - (c) large and negative.
    - (d) cannot be determined from the information given

7. If the sum of the paired differences between the Z scores on X and the (p. 171)
   Z scores on Y is close to 4.0, its maximum possible value, the correlation
   between X and Y is:
   (a) approximately zero.
   (b) large and positive.
   * (c) large and negative.
   (d) cannot be determined from the information given

8. The smallest and largest possible values of the Pearson r correlation (p. 170)
   coefficient are:
   (a) minus infinity and plus infinity.
   (b) 0 and 4.0.
   (c) −4.0 and +4.0.
   * (d) −1.0 and +1.0.

9. Which of the following indicates a *stronger* relationship between the two (p. 170)
   variables?
   * (a) −.54
   (b) .31
   (c) *Both* of the above indicate an equally strong relationship.

10. Which of the following indicates a *stronger* relationship between the two (p. 170)
    variables?
    (a) −.46
    (b) .46
    * (c) *Both* of the above indicate an equally strong relationship.

11. If we compute the correlation between scores on an intelligence test and (p. 175)
    grades in school, the correlation will be closest to zero for which of the
    following samples?
    (a) Children chosen randomly from the population
    * (b) Gifted children with IQs of at least 130
    (c) Children from the fourth through the eighth grades
    (d) Children with IQs between 90 and 130

12. It is more difficult to obtain a highly positive or a highly negative correlation (p. 175)
    between two variables when:
    * (a) the variability on both variables is extremely low.
    (b) the variability on both variables is extremely high.
    (c) the means of the raw scores of the two variables are similar.
    (d) the means of the raw scores of the two variables are very different.

13. When using the Pearson r as an inferential statistic, the correct statistical (p. 176)
    model to use is:
    (a) the normal curve.
    * (b) the t distribution.
    (c) chi square.
    (d) *none* of the above

14. A researcher finds that a correlation of .47 is statistically significant using (p. 177)
    the .05 criterion. The researcher should conclude that the population
    correlation coefficient is:
    (a) equal to zero.
    * (b) greater than zero.
    (c) equal to .47.
    (d) .47 or more.

15. A researcher finds that a correlation of .32 is *not* statistically significant (p. 177)
    using the .05 criterion. The researcher should conclude that the population
    correlation coefficient is:
    (a) equal to zero.
    (b) likely to be small and positive.
    (c) equal to .32.
    * (d) *none* of the above

16. A researcher finds that a correlation of −.51 is statistically significant using (p. 177)
    the .05 criterion. The researcher should conclude that the population
    correlation coefficient is:
    (a) equal to zero.
    * (b) less than zero.
    (c) equal to −.51.
    (d) −.51 or less.

17. A researcher finds that a correlation of .48 is *not* statistically significant (p. 177)
    using the .05 criterion. The researcher should conclude that:
    (a) the two variables are *not* linearly correlated.
    (b) the two variables are positively correlated, but only to a slight degree.
    (c) the two variables are positively correlated.
    * (d) there is not sufficient reason to believe that the two variables are linearly
        correlated.

18. The Pearson r detects relationships that are: (p. 177)
    * (a) only linear.
    (b) only curvilinear.
    (c) *both* linear and curvilinear.
    (d) *neither* linear nor curvilinear.

19. Using a sample of 10,000 cases, a researcher obtains a Pearson r of .11 (p. 178)
    that is statistically significant using the .05 criterion. The researcher should
    conclude that there is a strong positive relationship between the two variables.
    (a) True
    * (b) False

20. If the Pearson r between X and Y is .47, this means that 47% of the (p. 178)
    variability on X is explained by the variability on Y.
    (a) True
    * (b) False

21. If the Pearson r between X and Y is .40, what percentage of the variability (p. 178)
    on X is explained by the variability on Y?
    * (a) 16%
    (b) 40%
    (c) 60%
    (d) 84%

22. An r^2 of –1.00 indicates: (p. 178)
    (a) a strong positive relationship between the two variables.
    (b) no relationship between the two variables.
    (c) a strong negative relationship between the two variables.
    * (d) an error in computation.

23. If a Pearson r is statistically significant, we can conclude that the (p. 177)
    relationship between the two variables in the population is:
    * (a) unlikely to be zero.
    (b) strongly positive or strongly negative.
    (c) *both* of the above
    (d) *neither of the above*

24. The amount of variability on X that is explained by variability on Y is given by: (p. 178)
    (a) r
    (b) 1 – r
    * (c) r^2
    (d) 1 – r^2

25. A correlation of .50 indicates a relationship that is twice as strong as a   (p. 178)
    correlation of .25.
    (a) True
    * (b) False

26. When using the Pearson r as an inferential statistic, the degrees of   (p. 176)
    freedom are equal to:
    (a) the number of scores minus one.
    (b) the number of scores minus two.
    (c) the number of pairs minus one.
    * (d) the number of pairs minus two.

27. When using the Pearson r, what assumption(s) must be made?   (p. 178)
    * (a) The two variables are linearly related.
    (b) The raw scores are normally distributed in each of the two populations.
    (c) *Both* of the above
    (d) *Neither* of the above

28. If a researcher obtains a Pearson r of −.32 and the critical value needed to   (p. 176)
    reject the null hypothesis is .26, what should the researcher decide,
    and what error might be made?
    (a) Retain the null hypothesis—Type I error.
    (b) Retain the null hypothesis—Type II error.
    * (c) Reject the null hypothesis—Type I error.
    (d) Reject the null hypothesis—Type II error.

29. If a researcher obtains a Pearson r of .21 and the critical value needed to   (p. 176)
    reject the null hypothesis is .26, what should the researcher decide,
    and what error might be made?
    (a) Retain the null hypothesis—Type I error.
    * (b) Retain the null hypothesis—Type II error.
    (c) Reject the null hypothesis—Type I error.
    (d) Reject the null hypothesis—Type II error.

30. A researcher theorizes that intelligence is *not* correlated with introversion-   (p. 177)
    extraversion. The researcher obtains a sample of 15 people and finds that the
    correlation between intelligence and introversion is .37. This Pearson r is *not*
    statistically significant, so the researcher concludes that her theory is supported.
    What is wrong with this research design?
    (a) No firm conclusions can be drawn because the probability of a Type II error is
        unknown.
    (b) The sample size is too small, making useful results unlikely.
    (c) A researcher's theory should usually *not* be identified with the null hypothesis.
    * (d) *All* of the above
    (e) *None* of the above—the researcher's conclusion is correct.

31. If the correlation between X and Y is .52, the correlation between Y and X is: (p.172)
    (a) −.52
    (b) 0
    * (c) .52
    (d) Cannot be determined from the information given

32. A researcher finds that the Pearson r between two variables is +1.17.   (p. 170)
    This indicates that:
    (a) there is a strong positive correlation between the two variables.
    (b) one of the variables is not normally distributed.
    (c) both of the variables are not normally distributed.
    * (d) an error in computation was made.

33. A researcher finds that the correlation between weight and satisfaction with   (p. 174)
    life in general is −.74, and this correlation is statistically significant using
    the .05 criterion. The researcher should conclude that:
    (a) being overweight makes people unhappy with life in general.
    (b) being unhappy with life in general causes people to become overweight.
    (c) *both* of the above
    * (d) *neither* of the above

34. A researcher finds that the correlation between job satisfaction and   (p. 174)
    productivity on the job is .42, and this correlation is statistically significant
    using the .05 criterion. The researcher should conclude that:
    (a) liking one's job causes a person to produce more.
    (b) producing more causes a person to like the job more.
    (c) *both* of the above
    * (d) *neither* of the above

35. On a psychological measure, high numerical scores indicate greater mental (p. 165)
    health. A psychotherapist counts the number of therapy sessions missed by
    each patient during a two-month period. The psychotherapist theorizes that
    patients who are mentally healthy will miss fewer sessions. The psychotherapist
    expects the correlation between mental health and number of sessions missed to be:
    (a) positive.
    (b) approximately zero.
    * (c) negative.
    (d) cannot be determined from the information given

36. The correlation between scores on a 100-point test and a measure of (p. 177)
    success on a job is +.27, which is *not* statistically significant using the .05
    criterion. Which of the following conclusions is justified?
    * (a) A person with a test score of 40 is just as likely to succeed on this job as a
          person with a test score of 97.
    (b) A person with a test score of 86 is slightly more likely to succeed on this job than
        a person with a test score of 80.
    (c) A person with a test score above 90 is likely to succeed on this job.
    (d) *All* of the above

37. If the critical value of r needed to reject the null hypothesis when using the .05 (p. 176)
    criterion of significance is .32, which of the following is statistically significant?
    * (a) r = −.47
    (b) r = .26
    (c) *Both* of the above
    (d) *Neither* of the above

38. According to linear regression, tall parents will on the average produce (p. 179)
    children who are:
    (a) taller than they are.
    (b) as tall as they are.
    * (c) less tall than they are.
    (d) *none* of the above

39. In the equation $Y' = b_{YX}X + a_{YX}$, the *slope* of the regression line is denoted by: (p. 179)
    (a) a_{YX}
    * (b) b_{YX}
    (c) X
    (d) Y'

40. In linear regression, the error in predicting Y is defined as: (p. 180)
    (a) X – Y
    (b) Y – X
    (c) X – X′
    * (d) Y – Y′

41. In linear regression, which symbol stands for the *predicted* scores on Y? (p. 179)
    (a) a_{YX}
    (b) b_{YX}
    (c) Y
    * (d) Y′

42. The linear regression line: (p. 181)
    (a) minimizes the sum of errors in prediction.
    * (b) minimizes the sum of squared errors in prediction.
    (c) maximizes the sum of errors in prediction.
    (d) maximizes the sum of squared errors in prediction.

43. A researcher wishes to use scores on X to predict scores on Y as accurately as possible. The researcher wants: (p. 181)
    (a) a_{YX} to be small.
    (b) b_{YX} to be small.
    (c) r_{YX} to be small.
    * (d) the sum of the squared Y – Y′ values to be small.

44. In linear regression, the sum of errors in prediction: (p. 182)
    (a) must be small for prediction to be accurate.
    (b) must be large for prediction to be accurate.
    (c) is smaller for larger samples.
    * (d) is always equal to zero.

45. To determine a linear regression line, you must have a sample that has scores on *both* the predictor (X) and the criterion (Y). (p. 183)
    * (a) True
    (b) False

46. A researcher wishes to use scores on X to predict scores on Y as accurately (p. 182)
    as possible. Which of the following would the researcher most prefer?
    (a) $a_{YX} = .73$
    (b) $a_{YX} = 0$
    * (c) $r_{YX} = -.57$
    (d) $r_{YX} = .38$

47. When we use linear regression to predict scores on X, which of the following (p. 186)
    must be the same as the corresponding value used when we predict scores
    on Y?
    (a) $a_{XY} = a_{YX}$
    (b) $b_{XY} = b_{YX}$
    * (c) $r_{XY} = r_{YX}$
    (d) *All* of the above
    (e) *None* of the above

48. The regression line used to predict scores on Y from scores on X is the (p. 186)
    same as the regression line used to predict scores on X from scores on Y.
    (a) True
    * (b) False

49. As the correlation between X and Y gets closer to –1.0 or +1.0, the amount (p. 186)
    of error in predicting scores on Y:
    * (a) becomes smaller.
    (b) remains the same.
    (c) becomes larger.
    (d) cannot be determined from the information given

50. In linear regression, the standard error of estimate for predicting Y is equal to: (p. 186)
    (a) the sum of $Y - Y'$.
    (b) the sum of the squared $Y - Y'$ values.
    * (c) the square root of the average of the squared $Y - Y'$ values.
    (d) the square of the correlation between X and Y.

51. The minimum and maximum values of the standard error of estimate are: (p. 186)
    (a) Minus infinity and plus infinity.
    (b) –1.0 and +1.0.
    (c) 0 and plus infinity.
    * (d) 0 and the standard deviation of Y.

52. A researcher wishes to predict scores on Y from scores on X as accurately (p. 187)
    as possible. The researcher would like the standard error of estimate to be:
    * (a) much smaller than the standard deviation of Y.
    (b) equal to the standard deviation of Y.
    (c) much greater than the standard deviation of Y.

53. Using linear regression, we will be able to predict scores on Y from scores (p. 187)
    on X more accurately if for each X score, the variability of Y scores is:
    * (a) small.
    (b) medium.
    (c) large.
    (d) equal to the overall standard deviation of the Y scores.

54. If an individual with a Z score on X of 2.0 is predicted by the linear (p. 184)
    regression line to have a Z score on Y of 1.0, the predicted score on
    Y for an individual with a Z score on X of 1.0 would be:
    (a) 0
    * (b) 0.5
    (c) 2.0
    (d) Cannot be determined from the information given

55. If the correlation between X and Y is *not* statistically significant, linear (p. 184)
    regression should *not* be used because it will make too many errors in
    prediction.
    * (a) True
    (b) False

Chapter 13

1. Compared with continuous scores, ranks provide: (p. 194)
    * (a) less information.
    (b) the same amount of information.
    (c) more information

2. The smallest and largest possible values of the Spearman rank-order correlation coefficient are: (pp. 195–196)
    (a) minus infinity and plus infinity.
    (b) −4.0 and +4.0.
    (c) 0 and 1.
    * (d) −1.0 and +1.0.

3. If Bill is ranked highest, and Mary, Richard, and Joan are all tied for second, what rank should be assigned to Mary, Richard, and Joan? (p. 195)
    (a) 2.0
    (b) 2.5
    * (c) 3.0
    (d) 3.5

4. If Ellen is ranked highest, James is ranked second highest, and Ruth and Steven are tied for third, what rank should be assigned to Ruth and Steven? (p. 195)
    (a) 2.5
    (b) 3.0
    * (c) 3.5
    (d) 4.0

5. Compared to the Pearson r, the significance test for the Spearman rank-order correlation coefficient is: (p. 196)
    * (a) less likely to reject a false null hypothesis.
    (b) more likely to reject a false null hypothesis.
    (c) more likely to retain a true null hypothesis.
    (d) *none* of the above

6. A researcher has two judges rank 20 patients according to their degree (p. 195)
   of psychopathology. The researcher would like the judges to be in substantial
   agreement. Which Spearman rank-order correlation coefficient for the judges'
   ratings would the researcher most prefer?
   (a) −.89
   (b) 0
   (c) .42
   * (d) .83

7. If we have continuous scores on two variables, converting the scores (pp. 194, 196)
   to ranks and computing the Spearman rank-order correlation coefficient:
   (a) is usually a bad idea because ranks convey less information.
   (b) may produce a better measure of correlation if one variable is highly skewed.
   * (c) *both* of the above
   (d) *neither* of the above

8. A researcher computes a Spearman rank-order correlation coefficient of .57. (p. 196)
   The critical value needed to reject the null hypothesis is .38. What should the
   researcher conclude about the population rank-order correlation coefficient?
   (a) It is equal to zero.
   * (b) It is greater than zero.
   (c) It is equal to .38.
   (d) *None* of the above

9. A researcher computes a Spearman rank-order correlation coefficient of .30. (p. 196)
   The critical value needed to reject the null hypothesis is .38. What should the
   researcher conclude about the population rank-order correlation coefficient?
   (a) It is equal to zero.
   (b) It is *not* equal to zero.
   (c) It is equal to .38.
   * (d) *None* of the above

10. A researcher computes a Spearman rank-order correlation coefficient of .26. (p. 196)
    The critical value needed to reject the null hypothesis is .38. The correct way
    to state the conclusion is:
    (a) the population correlation coefficient is equal to zero.
    (b) the population correlation coefficient is *not* equal to zero.
    (c) the population correlation coefficient is .26.
    * (d) there is not sufficient reason to believe that the population correlation coefficient
      is not zero.

11. Which correlation coefficient should be used if one variable is continuous (p. 196)
    and one variable is genuinely dichotomous?
    (a) Biserial
    (b) Phi
    * (c) Point biserial
    (d) Tetrachoric

12. Which correlation coefficient should be used if both variables are genuinely (p. 201)
    dichotomous?
    (a) Biserial
    * (b) Phi
    (c) Point biserial
    (d) Tetrachoric

13. If we wish to compute the correlation between gender (male-female) and (p. 196)
    scores on an intelligence test, which correlation coefficient should we use?
    (a) Biserial
    (b) Phi
    * (c) Point biserial
    (d) Tetrachoric

14. The correlation between gender (male-female) and scores on an English test (p. 198)
    is –.62. If the critical value needed to reject the null hypothesis is .44, and if
    women were assigned a score of 0 and men were assigned a score of 1,
    what should we conclude?
    (a) Men and women are equal in English ability.
    (b) There is not sufficient reason to believe that men and women differ in English
        ability.
    (c) Men are superior to women in English ability.
    * (d) Women are superior to men in English ability.

15. The correlation between gender (male-female) and scores on an English (p. 198)
    test is .24. If the critical value needed to reject the null hypothesis is .44,
    and if women were assigned a score of 1 and men were assigned a score
    of 0, what should we conclude?
    (a) Men and women are equal in English ability.
    * (b) There is not sufficient reason to believe that men and women differ in English
        ability.
    (c) Men are slightly better than women in English ability.
    (d) Women are slightly better than men in English ability.

16. When performing a t test for the difference between two means, which of the following should be converted to a point biserial correlation coefficient? (p. 199)
    * (a) Only statistically significant values of t
    (b) Only values of t that are *not* statistically significant
    (a) *Both* of the above
    (d) *Neither* of the above

17. If the t test for the difference between two means is statistically significant and the corresponding point biserial correlation coefficient is .09, this indicates that: (p. 199)
    (a) the result is likely to be useful for practical purposes.
    * (b) the result is *not* likely to be useful for practical purposes.
    (c) the experiment should be repeated with a larger sample.
    (d) an error in computation was made.

18. If the t test for the difference between two means is statistically significant and the corresponding point biserial correlation coefficient is .47, this indicates that: (p. 200)
    * (a) the result is likely to be useful for practical purposes.
    (b) the result is *not* likely to be useful for practical purposes.
    (c) the experiment should be repeated with a larger sample.
    (d) an error in computation was made.

Questions 19–23 refer to the research study described below:

A researcher wishes to test the theory that taking a small amount of caffeine improves performance on a mathematics test. The researcher obtains two samples of 50 subjects, and the results are:

    Mean test score of group receiving caffeine = 81.7
    Mean test score of group receiving a placebo (pill with *no* caffeine) = 72.8

The t test for the difference between two means is statistically significant using the .05 criterion.

19. If the researcher converts t to a point biserial correlation coefficient and obtains a value of .57, what should the researcher conclude? (p. 200)
    (a) Caffeine has a very weak effect on test scores, so taking caffeine is *not* a good idea.
    * (b) Caffeine has a moderately strong effect on test scores, so taking caffeine *is* a good idea.
    (c) Taking caffeine has *no* effect on test scores.
    (d) No conclusions can be drawn.

20. If the researcher converts t to a point biserial correlation coefficient and (p. 200)
    obtains a value of .11 what should the researcher conclude?
    * (a) Caffeine has a very weak effect on test scores, so taking caffeine is *not* a good idea.
    (b) Caffeine has a moderately strong effect on test scores, so taking caffeine *is* a good idea.
    (c) Taking caffeine has *no* effect on test scores.
    (d) No conclusions can be drawn.

21. If the researcher converts t to a point biserial correlation, the point biserial (p. 200)
    correlation must be statistically significant because t is statistically significant.
    * (a) True
    (b) False

22. If the t in this study was *not* statistically significant, the researcher should (p. 199)
    not convert it to a point biserial correlation coefficient.
    * (a) True
    (b) False

23. If the researcher does *not* convert the value of t to a point biserial (p. 200)
    correlation coefficient and argues that taking caffeine is a good way
    to improve test scores because the results were statistically significant,
    what error might the researcher be making?
    (a) Underestimating the effect of caffeine on test scores
    * (b) Overestimating the effect of caffeine on test scores
    (c) A Type II error
    (d) *None* of the above—the researcher is correct

24. The smallest and largest possible values or the point biserial correlation (p. 196)
    coefficient are:
    (a) minus infinity and plus infinity.
    (b) –4.0 and +4.0.
    (c) 0 and 1.
    * (d) –1.0 and +1.0.

25. A researcher computes a point biserial correlation of –.47. The critical (p. 198)
    value needed to reject the null hypothesis is .30. What should the researcher
    conclude about the population point biserial correlation coefficient?
    (a) It is equal to zero.
    * (b) It is less than zero.
    (c) It is equal to –.47.
    (d) *None* of the above

26. A researcher computes a point biserial correlation coefficient of .21. (p. 198)
    The critical value needed to reject the null hypothesis is .30. What should
    the researcher conclude about the population point biserial correlation coefficient?
    (a) It is equal to zero.
    (b) It is greater than zero.
    (c) It is equal to .21.
    * (d) *None* of the above

27. A researcher computes a point biserial correlation coefficient of .19. The (p. 198)
    critical value needed to reject the null hypothesis is .30. The correct
    way to state the conclusion is:
    (a) the population correlation coefficient is equal to zero.
    (b) the population correlation coefficient is *not* equal to zero.
    (c) the population correlation coefficient is .19.
    * (d) there is not sufficient reason to believe that the population correlation coefficient
        is not zero.

28. The formula for the Pearson r correlation coefficient gives the same (pp. 195, 197)
    result as which of the following?
    (a) The Spearman rank-order correlation coefficient when there are no tied ranks
    (b) The point biserial correlation coefficient
    * (c) *Both* of the above
    (d) *Neither* of the above

29. If one variable is continuous, and the other variable is dichotomous but its (p. 201)
    underlying distribution is normal, which correlation coefficient should be used?
    * (a) Biserial
    (b) Phi
    (c) Point biserial
    (d) Tetrachoric

30. If both variables are dichotomous but their underlying distributions are (p. 201)
    normal, which correlation coefficient should be used?
    (a) Biserial
    (b) Phi
    (c) Point biserial
    * (d) Tetrachoric

Chapter 14

1. The *power* of a statistical test is defined as the probability of: (p. 205)
    (a) retaining a false null hypothesis.
    (b) retaining a true null hypothesis.
  * (c) rejecting a false null hypothesis.
    (d) rejecting a true null hypothesis.

2. If the power of a statistical test is .80, which of the following is equal to .80? (p. 205)
    (a) The probability of a Type I error
    (b) The probability of a Type II error
    (c) 1.0 minus the probability of a Type I error
  * (d) 1.0 minus the probability of a Type II error

3. If the power of a statistical test is .80 and the .05 criterion of significance is used, what is the probability of a Type II error? (p. 205)
    (a) .05
  * (b) .20
    (c) .80
    (d) Cannot be determined from the information given

4. A researcher who wants to draw inferences about one or more populations as accurately as possible would like the power of the statistical test to be: (p. 205)
    (a) small.
    (b) medium.
  * (c) high.
    (d) equal to the criterion of significance.

5. If a researcher conducts a study where the power of the statistical test is low, this indicates that: (p. 205)
    (a) the probability of a Type I error is low.
    (b) the probability of a Type II error is low.
    (c) the probability of *both* a Type I error and a Type II error is low.
  * (d) the study is likely to be a waste of time and effort.

6. If a researcher conducts a study where the power of the statistical test is low, which of the following is likely to occur? (p. 205)
   * (a) A false negative—erroneously concluding that the researcher's theory was *not* supported
   (b) A false positive—erroneously concluding that the researcher's theory was supported
   (c) *Both* of the above are equally likely.
   (d) *Neither* of the above is likely.

7. If the power of a statistical test is .25 and the .05 criterion of significance is used, what is the probability of a Type II error? (p. 205)
   (a) .05
   (b) .25
   * (c) .75
   (d) Cannot be determined from the information given

8. The power of a statistical test is equal to the probability of: (p. 205)
   (a) a Type I error.
   (b) a Type II error.
   * (c) getting a result that is statistically significant.
   (d) getting a result that is *not* statistically significant.

9. If we don't know the power of a statistical test: (p. 205)
   * (a) we cannot draw any conclusions from retaining the null hypothesis.
   (b) we cannot draw any conclusions from rejecting the null hypothesis.
   (c) *both* of the above
   (d) *neither* of the above

10. If the null hypothesis is actually false, why is there a chance that we will fail to reject it? (p. 205)
    (a) Sampling error may cause the sample(s) in a study to be unrepresentative of the population from which they were drawn.
    (b) We can measure only a small part of the population(s) in which we are interested.
    * (c) *Both* of the above
    (d) *Neither* of the above

11. According to the textbook, most research in the behavioral sciences reports the power of the statistical tests that are used. (p. 205)
    (a) True
    * (b) False

12. If we switch from the .05 criterion of significance to the .01 criterion, the power of the statistical test: (p. 206)
    * (a) becomes smaller.
    (b) remains the same.
    (c) becomes larger.
    (d) cannot be determined from the information given

13. As the sample size becomes larger, the power of the statistical test: (p. 206)
    (a) becomes smaller.
    (b) remains the same.
    * (c) becomes larger.
    (d) cannot be determined from the information given

14. Which of the following will *increase* the power of a statistical test? (p. 206)
    (a) Switching from the .05 criterion of significance to the .01 criterion
    (b) Decreasing the sample size
    * (c) Increasing the sample size
    (d) *None* of the above

15. The *population effect size* refers to: (p. 206)
    * (a) how false the null hypothesis is.
    (b) how false the alternative hypothesis is.
    (c) the probability of a Type II error.
    (d) the relationship between the criterion of significance and the power of the statistical test.

16. As the effect size becomes larger, the power of the statistical test: (p. 206)
    (a) becomes smaller.
    (b) remains the same.
    * (c) becomes larger.
    (d) cannot be determined from the information given

17. For which of the following will the power of the statistical test be the *largest*? (p. 206)
    (a) .01 criterion of significance, N = 30, effect size is small
    (b) .05 criterion of significance, N = 50, effect size is small
    (c) .01 criterion of significance, N = 30, effect size is large
    * (d) .05 criterion of significance, N = 50, effect size is large

18. For which of the following are we most likely to commit a Type II error? (p. 206)
    * (a) .01 criterion of significance, N = 30, effect size is small
    (b) .05 criterion of significance, N = 50, effect size is small
    (c) .01 criterion of significance, N = 30, effect size is large
    (d) .05 criterion of significance, N = 50, effect size is large

19. When performing a power analysis, which of the following is an (pp. 207–208)
    acceptable *alternative* hypothesis?
    (a) The population mean is *not* equal to zero.
    * (b) The population mean is 2 points above or below zero.
    (c) *Both* of the above
    (d) *Neither* of the above

20. When performing a power analysis, which of the following is used? (p. 209)
    * (a) Only population values
    (b) Only the results obtained from one or more samples
    (c) *Both* of the above
    (d) *Neither of the above*

21. A researcher tests the null hypothesis that the mean of one population is (p. 209)
    100.0 against the alternative hypothesis that the population mean is either
    95 or 105. If the power of the statistical test is 87, which of the following
    conclusions is justified?
    (a) The power of the statistical test is acceptably high.
    (b) The probability of a Type II error if the population mean is 95 or 105 is .13.
    * (c) *Both* of the above
    (d) *Neither* of the above

22. A researcher tests the null hypothesis that the mean of one population is (p. 209)
    100.0 against the alternative hypothesis that the population mean is either
    95 or 105. If the power of the statistical test is .38, which of the following
    conclusions is justified?
    (a) The power of the statistical test is acceptably high.
    * (b) The probability of a Type II error if the population mean is 95 or 105 is .62.
    (c) *Both* of the above
    (d) *Neither* of the above

23. When determining the sample size that will give a statistical test adequate (p. 211)
    power, it is recommended that the desired power be set at:
    (a) .05
    * (b) .80
    (c) .95
    (d) .99

24. A researcher tests the null hypothesis that the proportion of one population   (p. 213)
    is .50 against the alternative hypothesis that the population proportion is
    either .45 or .55. If the power of the statistical test is .84, which of the following
    conclusions is justified?
    * (a) The power of the statistical test is acceptably high.
    (b) The probability of a Type II error if the population proportion is .45 or .55 is .84.
    (c) *Both* of the above
    (d) *Neither* of the above

25. A researcher tests the null hypothesis that the proportion of one population   (p. 213)
    is .50 against the alternative hypothesis that the population proportion is
    either .45 or .55. If the power of the statistical test is .05, which of
    the following conclusions is justified?
    (a) The power of the statistical test is acceptably high.
    (b) The probability of a Type II error if the population proportion is .45 or .55 is .05.
    (c) *Both* of the above
    * (d) *Neither* of the above

26. A researcher tests the null hypothesis that the population value of a   (p.215)
    Pearson r correlation coefficient is zero against the alternative hypothesis
    that the population correlation is either −.30 or +.30. If the power of the
    statistical test is .90, which of the following conclusions is justified?
    (a) The power of the statistical test is acceptably high.
    (b) The probability of a Type II error if the population correlation is −.30 or +.30 is .10.
    * (c) *Both* of the above
    (d) *Neither* of the above

27. A researcher tests the null hypothesis that the population value of a   (p. 215)
    Pearson r correlation coefficient is zero against the alternative hypothesis
    that the population correlation is either −.30 or +.30. If the power of the
    statistical test is .20, which of the following conclusions is justified?
    (a) The power of the statistical test is acceptably high.
    (b) The probability of a Type II error if the population correlation is −.30 or +.30 is .80.
    * (c) *Both* of the above
    (d) *Neither* of the above

28. A researcher tests the null hypothesis that the difference between two (p. 217)
    population means is zero against the alternative hypothesis that the
    population means are 1 standard deviation apart. If the power of the
    statistical test is .85, which of the following conclusions is justified?
    * (a) The power of the statistical test is acceptably high.
    (b) The probability of a Type II error if the two population means are 1 standard
        deviation apart is .85.
    (c) *Both* of the above
    (d) *Neither* of the above

29. A researcher tests the null hypothesis that the difference between two (p. 217)
    population means is zero against the alternative hypothesis that the
    population means are 1 standard deviation apart. If the power of the
    statistical test is .10, which of the following conclusions is justified?
    (a) The power of the statistical test is acceptably high.
    (b) The probability of a Type II error if the two population means are 1 standard
        deviation apart is .10.
    (c) *Both* of the above
    * (d) *Neither* of the above

30. If the sample size determination for a statistical test indicates that a sample (p. 214)
    of 120 is needed to have power equal to .80, and the researcher uses a
    sample of 50, what is likely to happen?
    * (a) A false negative—erroneously concluding that the researcher's theory was *not*
        supported
    (b) A false positive—erroneously concluding that the researcher's theory was supported
    (c) *Both* of the above are equally likely.
    (d) *Neither* of the above is likely.

Chapter 15

1. A researcher wishes to test the differences among five population (pp. 224–225)
   means, using the .05 criterion of significance. Why is it a bad idea to
   perform 10 t tests for the 10 pairs of means—population 1 versus
   population 2, population 1 versus population 3, and so on?
   - (a) The probability of making at least one Type I error will be greater than .05.
   - (b) It's too likely that the researcher will get some statistically significant results purely by chance.
   - * (c) *Both* of the above
   - (d) *Neither* of the above

2. If we test the difference between *two* population means, one-way analysis of (p. 225)
   variance and the t test for the difference between two means will yield
   identical results.
   - * (a) True
   - (b) False

3. A researcher who wishes to test the difference among three or more (pp. 224–225)
   population means should use:
   - (a) the normal curve model.
   - (b) the standard error of the mean.
   - (c) the t test for the difference between two means.
   - * (d) one-way analysis of variance.

4. In one-way analysis of variance, which of the following is the *error variance*? (p. 225)
   - (a) The between-group variance
   - * (b) The within-group variance
   - (c) The total variance
   - (d) *None* of the above

5. In one-way analysis of variance, what can cause subjects within the same (p. 226)
   group to vary?
   - (a) The variable whose effects are being studied by the researcher
   - * (b) Irrelevant factors such as sampling error
   - (c) *Both* of the above
   - (d) *Neither* of the above

6. In one-way analysis of variance, what can cause the group means to vary? (p. 226)
   (a) The variable whose effects are being studied by the researcher
   (b) Irrelevant factors such as sampling error
   * (c) *Both* of the above
   (d) *Neither* of the above

7. In one-way analysis of variance, *within-group variance* refers to: (p. 225)
   (a) The variability of the group means
   * (b) The variability of the scores in each group
   (c) The total variability of all the scores

8. In one-way analysis or variance, *between-group variance* refers to: (p. 225)
   * (a) the variability of the group means.
   (b) the variability of the scores in each group.
   (c) the total variability of all the scores.

9. Questions 9–19 refer to the two research studies summarized below:

	Study 1			Study 2	
Group 1	Group 2	Group 3	Group 1	Group 2	Group 3
7	12	4	7	12	9
5	12	0	12	5	6
6	9	2	0	2	4

10. In which study is the within-group variance larger? (p. 226)
    (a) Study 1
    * (b) Study 2
    (c) It is equal in both studies.

11. In which study is the between-group variance larger? (p. 226)
    * (a) Study 1
    (b) Study 2
    (c) It is equal in both studies.

12. In which study is the total variance larger? (p. 226)
    (a) Study 1
    (b) Study 2
    * (c) It is equal in both studies.

13. In Study 1, what can cause the score of 7 and the score of 5 in Group 1 (p. 226)
to be different?
   (a) The variable whose effects are being studied by the researcher
   * (b) Irrelevant factors such as sampling error
   (c) *Both* of the above
   (d) *Neither* of the above

14. In Study 2, what can cause the score of 12 and the score of 0 in Group 1 to (p. 226)
be different?
   (a) The variable whose effects are being studied by the researcher
   * (b) Irrelevant factors such as sampling error
   (c) *Both* of the above
   (d) *Neither* of the above

15. In Study 1, the mean of Group 1 is 6.0 and the mean of Group 2 is 11.0. (p. 226)
What can cause these means to be different?
   (a) The variable whose effects are being studied by the researcher
   (b) Irrelevant factors such as sampling error
   * (c) *Both* of the above
   (d) *Neither* of the above

16. In Study 2, the means of Groups 1, 2, and 3 are the same (6.33). This (p. 226)
indicates that the results of this study *cannot* be statistically significant.
   * (a) True
   (b) False

17. Which study is more likely to yield statistically significant results? (p. 226)
   * (a) Study 1
   (b) Study 2
   (c) Both studies are equally likely to yield statistically significant results.

18. A researcher who hopes to obtain statistically significant results would prefer: (p. 226)
   (a) large differences between the scores in each group, such as 12 and 0 in Group 1 of Study 2.
   * (b) large differences between the means of each group, as in Study 1.
   (c) *both* of the above
   (d) *neither* of the above

19. A researcher who hopes to obtain statistically significant results would prefer: (p. 226)
    * (a) small differences between the scores in each group, such as 7 and 5 in Group 1 of Study 1.
    (b) small differences between the means of each group, as in Study 2.
    (c) *both* of the above
    (d) *neither* of the above

20. In one-way analysis of variance, the correct statistical model to use is: (p. 228)
    (a) the normal curve.
    (b) the t distributions.
    (c) chi square.
    * (d) the F distributions.

21. In one-way analysis of variance, the degrees of freedom between groups is equal to: (p. 231)
    (a) the number of scores.
    (b) the number of groups.
    (c) the number of scores minus one.
    * (d) the number of groups minus one.

22. In one-way analysis of variance, mean squares are obtained by: (p. 231)
    (a) dividing each sum of squares by the number of scores.
    (b) dividing each sum of squares by the number of groups.
    (c) dividing each sum of squares by the number of scores minus one.
    * (d) dividing each sum of squares by the associated degrees of freedom.

23. In one-way analysis of variance, the F ratio is computed by: (p. 232)
    (a) dividing the sum of squares between groups by the sum of squares within groups.
    (b) dividing the sum of squares within groups by the sum of squares between groups.
    * (c) dividing the mean square between groups by the mean square within groups.
    (d) dividing the mean square within groups by the mean square between groups.

24. The smallest and largest possible values of F are: (p. 233)
    (a) minus infinity and plus infinity.
    (b) −1.0 and +1.0.
    (c) 0 and 1.0.
    * (d) 0 and plus infinity.

25. In one-way analysis of variance, if the null hypothesis is true, what value of F should we expect? (p. 233)
    (a) 0
    * (b) 1.0
    (c) The standard deviation of the raw scores
    (d) The total variance divided by the number of scores minus one

26. All of the F distributions are: (p. 233)
    (a) unimodal and symmetric.
    (b) unimodal and negatively skewed.
    * (c) unimodal and positively skewed.
    (d) bimodal and symmetric.

27. In order to perform a one-way analysis of variance, the sizes of all of the samples must be equal. (p. 234)
    (a) True
    * (b) False

28. In one-way analysis of variance, multiple comparisons should be used only if the results are statistically significant. (p. 236)
    * (a) True
    (b) False

29. Why are multiple comparisons used in one-way analysis of variance? (p. 236)
    * (a) To determine which population means differ from each other
    (b) To determine the probability of a Type I error
    (c) To determine the probability of a Type II error
    (d) To determine the power of the statistical test

30. A researcher conducts a one-way analysis of variance using four groups. The group means are: Group 1, 12.7; Group 2, 5.6; Group 3, 8.9; Group 4, 6.2. If the F test is statistically significant, the researcher should conclude that: (p. 236)
    (a) the mean of population 1 is different from the mean of population 2.
    (b) the means of all four populations are different from one another.
    (c) the mean of population 1 is *not* zero.
    * (d) the means of all four populations are not exactly equal.

31. Using a one-way analysis of variance with three groups, a researcher obtains (p. 237) a statistically significant F ratio. The group means are: Group 1, 76.3; Group 2, 70.1; Group 3, 74.2. If a protected t test indicates that LSD = 3.1, the researcher should conclude that which population means are different?
    (a) Only population 1 and population 2
    (b) Population 1 and 2 *and* population 1 and 3
    * (c) Population 1 and 2 *and* population 2 and 3
    (d) Population 1 and 2, population 1 and 3, *and* population 2 and 3

32. Using a one-way analysis of variance with three groups, a researcher obtains (p. 237) a statistically significant F ratio. The group means are: Group 1, 25.8; Group 2, 15.4; Group 3, 20.6. If a protected t test indicates that LSD = 9.7, the researcher should conclude that which population means are different?
    * (a) Only population 1 and population 2
    (b) Population 1 and 2 *and* population 1 and 3
    (c) Population 1 and 2 *and* population 2 and 3
    (d) Population 1 and 2, population 1 and 3, *and* population 2 and 3

33. In one-way analysis of variance, the protected t test should not be used if (p. 237) there are six or more groups.
    * (a) True
    (b) False

34. Using a one-way analysis of variance with three groups, a researcher (p. 238) obtains a statistically significant F ratio. For which of the following confidence intervals, obtained from the protected t test, should the researcher conclude that the corresponding population means are not equal?
    (a) Group 1 versus group 2: –6.7 to 8.89
    (b) Group 1 versus group 3: –5.3 to 1.02
    * (c) Group 2 versus group 3: 3.1 to 8.01
    (d) *All* of the above
    (e) *None* of the above

35. Using a one-way analysis of variance with three groups, a researcher obtains (p. 238) a statistically significant F ratio. For which of the following confidence intervals, obtained from the protected t test, should the researcher conclude that the corresponding population means are at least 4 points apart?
    (a) Group 1 versus group 2: –7.2 to 5.8
    (b) Group 1 versus group 3: 0.6 to 9.4
    * (c) Group 2 versus group 3: 4.7 to 8.8
    (d) *All* of the above
    (e) *None* of the above

36. Using a one-way analysis of variance with three groups, a researcher obtains (p. 237)
    a statistically significant F ratio. If the mean of Group 1 is 16.8 and the mean of
    Group 2 is 10.2, and a protected t test indicates that LSD = 5.0, what should
    the researcher conclude about the means of populations 1 and 2?
    (a) They are equal.
    * (b) They are *not* equal.
    (c) They are 5 points apart.
    (d) They are at least 6.6 points apart.

37. Using a one-way analysis of variance with three groups, a researcher obtains (p. 237)
    a statistically significant F ratio. If the mean of Group 1 is 25.7 and the mean of
    Group 2 is 20.4, and a protected t test indicates that LSD = 8.0, what should the
    researcher conclude about the means of populations 1 and 2?
    (a) They are equal.
    (b) They are *not* equal.
    (c) They are *not* 8 points apart.
    * (d) *None* of the above

38. Using a one-way analysis of variance with three groups, a researcher obtains (p. 237)
    a statistically significant F ratio. If the mean of Group 1 is 20.8 and the mean
    of Group 2 is 23.4, and a protected t test indicates that LSD = 4.0, the correct
    way to state the conclusion about the means of populations 1 and 2 is:
    (a) they are equal.
    (b) they are *not* equal.
    (c) they are no more than 4 points apart.
    * (d) there is not sufficient reason to reject the hypothesis that they are equal.

39. Using a one-way analysis of variance with three groups, a researcher obtains (p. 238)
    a statistically significant F ratio. For which of the following confidence intervals
    would a protected t test *reject* the hypothesis that the corresponding population
    means are equal?
    (a) 0.6 to 9.4
    (b) 4.7 to 8.8
    * (c) *Both* of the above
    (d) *Neither* of the above

40. If the sample sizes are approximately equal, one-way analysis of variance will (p. 239)
    not give accurate results if which of the following assumptions is violated?
    * (a) The observations must be independent.
    (b) The variances must be equal for all treatment populations.
    (c) The raw scores in each population must be normally distributed.

41. A one-way analysis of variance is conducted using four groups. In order for the F ratio to be statistically significant, all of the four group means must be significantly different from one another. (p. 237)
    (a) True
    * (b) False

42. Entering the F table with 4 degrees of freedom in the numerator and 20 degrees of freedom in the denominator will yield the same F values as entering the table with 20 degrees of freedom in the numerator and 4 degrees of freedom in the denominator. (p. 234)
    (a) True
    * (b) False

43. If the F ratio in a one-way analysis of variance is 4.72 and the critical value needed to reject the null hypothesis is 3.48, what decision should the researcher make and what error might he made? (p. 234)
    (a) Retain the null hypothesis—Type I error.
    (b) Retain the null hypothesis—Type II error.
    * (c) Reject the null hypothesis—Type I error.
    (d) Reject the null hypothesis—Type II error.

44. If the F ratio in a one-way analysis of variance is 2.19 and the critical value needed to reject the null hypothesis is 3.48, what decision should the researcher make and what error might be made? (p. 234)
    (a) Retain the null hypothesis—Type I error.
    * (b) Retain the null hypothesis—Type II error.
    (c) Reject the null hypothesis—Type I error.
    (d) Reject the null hypothesis—Type II error.

45. Which of the following should be converted to epsilon? (p. 239)
    * (a) Only statistically significant values of F
    (b) Only values of F that are *not* statistically significant
    (c) *Both* of the above
    (d) *Neither* of the above

46. If an F ratio is statistically significant and the corresponding epsilon is .14, this indicates that: (p. 239)
    (a) the result is likely to be useful for practical purposes.
    * (b) the result is *not* likely to be useful for practical purposes.
    (c) the study should be repeated with a larger sample.
    (d) an error in computation was made.

47. If an F ratio is statistically significant and the corresponding epsilon is .52, (p. 239)
this indicates that:
* (a) the result is likely to be useful for practical purposes.
   (b) the result is *not* likely to be useful for practical purposes.
   (c) the study should be repeated with a larger sample.
   (d) an error in computation was made.

48. An F value of –0.97 indicates: (p. 232)
   (a) the results are statistically significant.
   (b) the results are *not* statistically significant.
   (c) one or more assumptions of the F test was violated.
* (d) an error in computation.

49. The critical value of F needed to reject the null hypothesis becomes (p. 233)
smaller as:
   (a) df_B decreases and df_W decreases.
   (b) df_B decreases and df_W increases.
   (c) df_B increases and df_W decreases.
* (d) df_B increases and df_W increases.

50. A value of F between 0 and +1.0: (p. 234)
   (a) indicates an error in computation.
* (b) cannot be statistically significant.
   (c) may be statistically significant if the sample size is very large.
   (d) may be statistically significant if there is a large number of groups.

Questions 51–55 refer to these data from a one-way analysis of variance:

Total Sum of squares = 38
Sum of Squares Between Groups = 14
Degrees of freedom between groups = 2
Degrees of freedom within groups = 12

51. The within-groups sum of squares is equal to: (p. 231)
   (a) 14
* (b) 24
   (c) 52
   (d) Cannot be determined from the information given

52. The mean square between groups is equal to: (p. 232)
    (a) 0.86
    (b) 1.17
    (c) 2.0
    * (d) 7.0

53. The mean square within groups is equal to: (p. 232)
    (a) 0.86
    (b) 1.17
    * (c) 2.0
    (d) 7.0

54. The F ratio is equal to: (p. 232)
    (a) 0.29
    (b) 0.74
    (c) 3.31
    * (d) 3.5

55. How many groups were used in this study? (p. 231)
    * (a) 3
    (b) 4
    (c) 5
    (d) Cannot be determined from the information given

Questions 56–60 refer to these data from a one-way analysis of variance:

>   Total Sum of Squares = 100
>   Sum of Squares Within Groups = 80
>   Number of groups = 5
>   Number of subjects = 25

56. The between-groups sum of squares is equal to: (p. 231)
    * (a) 20
    (b) 80
    (c) 180
    (d) Cannot be determined from the information given

57. The degrees of freedom between groups is equal to: (p. 231)
    * (a) 4
    (b) 20
    (c) 24
    (d) Cannot be determined from the information given

58. The mean square between groups is equal to: (p. 232)
    (a) .80
    (b) 1.0
    (c) 4.0
    * (d) 5.0

59. The mean square within groups is equal to: (p. 232)
    (a) 3.2
    * (b) 4.0
    (c) 16.0
    (d) 20.0

60. The F ratio is equal to: (p. 232)
    (a) .04
    (b) .25
    (c) .80
    * (d) 1.25

Chapter 16

1. A researcher who wants to study the relationship of two or more independent variables to a dependent variable should use: (p. 244)
    - (a) the standard error of the mean.
    - (b) the t test for the difference between two means.
    - (c) one-way analysis of variance.
    - * (d) two-way analysis of variance.

2. How does a two-way analysis of variance *differ* from a one-way analysis of variance? (p. 245)
    - * (a) More than one null hypothesis is tested.
    - (b) There is no within-group variation.
    - (c) *Both* of the above
    - (d) *Neither* of the above

3. How does a two-way analysis of variance *differ* from a one-way analysis of variance? (p. 244)
    - (a) Three F tests are performed.
    - (b) Between-groups variation is divided into variation due to factor 1, factor 2, and interaction.
    - * (c) *Both* of the above
    - (d) *Neither* of the above

4. *ALL* of the following are true about *both* one-way analysis of variance and two-way analysis of variance *EXCEPT*: (pp. 244–245)
    - (a) the total variance is divided into between-group variation and within-group variation.
    - (b) within-groups variation represents error variation.
    - (c) the correct statistical model to use is the F distributions.
    - * (d) between-groups variation is divided into variation due to factor 1, factor 2, and interaction.

5. In two-way analysis of variance, which of the following is the *error variance*? (p. 244)
    - (a) The between-group variation
    - * (b) The within-group variation
    - (c) The variation due to interaction
    - (d) The total variation

6. In two-way analysis of variance, what can cause subjects within the same group to vary? (p. 244)
   (a) The variable whose effects are being studied by the researcher
   * (b) Irrelevant factors such as sampling error
   (c) *Both* of the above
   (d) *Neither* of the above

7. In two-way analysis of variance, *within-group variance* refers to: (p. 244)
   (a) the variability of the group means.
   * (b) the variability of the scores in each group.
   (c) the total variability of all the scores.

8. In two-way analysis of variance, *between-group variance* refers to: (p. 244)
   * (a) the variability of the group means.
   (b) the variability of the scores in each group.
   (c) the total variability of all the scores.

Questions 9–25 refer to the two research studies summarized below, where men and women were given a high or low dose of caffeine and then took a 10-point mathematics quiz:

Study 1

Factor 1: Caffeine Dose

		High	Low
Factor 2: Gender	Male	9 10 8	0 1 2
	Female	6 8 7	3 4 2

Study 2

Factor 1: Caffeine Dose

		High	Low
Factor 2: Gender	Male	10 3 2	4 9 2
	Female	8 1 6	7 0 8

9. In which study is the within-group variance larger? (p. 247)
   (a) Study 1
   * (b) Study 2
   (c) It is equal in both studies.

10. In which study is the total variance larger? (p. 246)
    (a) Study 1
    (b) Study 2
    * (c) It is equal in both studies.

11. In which study is the variation due to factor 1 larger? (p. 247)
    * (a) Study 1
    (b) Study 2
    (c) It is equal in both studies.

12. In which study is the variation due to factor 2 larger? (p. 248)
    (a) Study 1
    (b) Study 2
    * (c) It is equal in both studies.

13. In Study 1, what can cause the score of 10 and the score of 9 to be different? (p. 247)
    (a) Caffeine dose
    (b) Gender
    * (c) Irrelevant factors such as sampling error
    (d) *All* of the above

14. In Study 2, what can cause the score of 7 and the score of 0 to be different? (p. 247)
    (a) Caffeine dose
    (b) Gender
    * (c) Irrelevant factors such as sampling error
    (d) *All* of the above

15. In Study 1, what can cause the score of 10 and the score of 6 to be different? (p. 247)
    (a) Only caffeine dose
    (b) Only gender
    (c) *Both* caffeine dose and irrelevant factors such as sampling error
    * (d) *Both* gender and irrelevant factors such as sampling error

16. In Study 1, what can cause the score of 10 and the score of 0 to be different? (p. 247)
    (a) Only caffeine dose
    (b) Only gender
    * (c) *Both* caffeine dose and irrelevant factors such as sampling error
    (d) *Both* gender and irrelevant factors such as sampling error

17. In Study 2, which of the following *cannot* cause the score of 10 and the (p. 247)
score of 1 to be different?
    * (a) Caffeine dose
    (b) Gender
    (c) Irrelevant factors such as sampling error

18. In Study 2, which of the following *cannot* cause the score of 1 and the (p. 247)
score of 7 to be different?
    (a) Caffeine dose
    * (b) Gender
    (c) Irrelevant factors such as sampling error

19. In Study 1, the mean of column 1 is 8.0 and the mean of column 2 is 2.0. (p. 247)
What can cause these means to be different?
    (a) Only caffeine dose
    (b) Only gender
    * (c) *Both* caffeine dose and irrelevant factors such as sampling error
    (d) *Both* gender and irrelevant factors such as sampling error

20. In Study 2, the mean of column 1 is 5.0 and the mean of column 2 is 5.0. (p. 247)
This indicates that the effects of caffeine *cannot* be statistically significant.
    * (a) True
    (b) False

21. Which study is more likely to yield statistically significant results for the (p. 250)
caffeine factor?
    * (a) Study 1
    (b) Study 2
    (c) Both studies are equally likely to yield statistically significant effects for caffeine.

22. Which study is more likely to yield statistically significant results for gender? (p. 250)
    (a) Study 1
    (b) Study 2
    * (c) Neither study is likely to yield a statistically significant result for gender.

23. A researcher who hopes to obtain statistically significant results would prefer: (p. 250)
    (a) large differences between the scores in each group, such as 10 and 3 in Study 2.
    * (b) large differences between the means of each group, as in the column means for Study 1.
    (c) *both* of the above
    (d) *neither* of the above

24. In Study 1, it is possible for the F test for caffeine to be statistically (p. 250)
significant and the F test for gender *not* to be statistically significant.
    * (a) True
    (b) False

25. In Study 2, the column means are equal and the row means are equal. (p. 250)
Therefore, this study *cannot* yield statistically significant results for either
caffeine or gender.
    * (a) True
    (b) False

26. In two-way analysis of variance, mean squares are obtained by: (p. 248)
    (a) dividing each sum of squares by the number of scores.
    (b) dividing each sum of squares by the number of groups.
    (c) dividing each sum of squares by the number of scores minus one.
    * (d) dividing each sum of squares by the associated degrees of freedom

27. In two-way analysis of variance, the denominator of every F test is: (p. 250)
    (a) the sum of squares between groups.
    (b) the sum of squares within groups.
    (c) the mean square between groups.
    * (d) the mean square within groups.

28. In two-way analysis of variance, a protected t test for either factor 1 or (p. 251)
factor 2 should be performed if and only if:
    (a) the F test for that factor is statistically significant.
    (b) the F test for the interaction is *not* statistically significant.
    * (c) *both* of the above
    (d) *neither* of the above

29. A researcher conducts a two-way analysis of variance. Only the F test for (p. 251)
factor 1 (columns) is statistically significant. The means of the three columns
are: Column 1, 5.6; Column 2, 9.4; Column 3, 1.2. If a protected t test indicates
that LSD = 3.2, the researcher should conclude that which population means
are different?
    (a) Only population 2 and population 3
    (b) Population 1 and 3 *and* population 2 and 3
    (c) Population 1 and 2 *and* population 2 and 3
    * (d) Population 1 and 2, population 1 and 3, *and* Population 2 and 3

30. A researcher conducts a two-way analysis of variance. Only the F test for (p. 250)
    factor 2 (rows) is statistically significant. The means of the three rows are:
    Row 1, 14.6; Row 2, 7.8; Row 3, 10.9. The researcher should conclude that:
    (a) the means of all three populations are different from one another.
    (b) the mean of population 1 is *not* zero.
    (c) the three populations differ by at least 6.8.
    * (d) the means of all three populations are not exactly equal to one another.

31. A researcher conducts a two-way analysis of variance. Only the F test for (p. 251)
    factor 2 (rows) is statistically significant. The means of the three rows are:
    Row 1, 42.5; Row 2, 47.8; Row 3, 51.5. If a protected t test indicates that
    LSD = 8.1, the researcher should conclude that which population means are different?
    * (a) Only population 1 and population 3
    (b) Population 1 and 2 *and* population 1 and 3
    (c) Population 1 and 2 *and* population 2 and 3
    (d) Population 1 and 2, population 1 and 3, *and* population 2 and 3

32. A researcher conducts a two-way analysis of variance. Only the F test for (p. 252)
    factor 1 (columns) is statistically significant. For which of the following
    confidence intervals, obtained from the protected t test, should the researcher
    conclude that the corresponding population means are *not* equal?
    (a) Group 1 versus group 2: −3.8 to 9.4
    * (b) Group 1 versus group 3: 1.7 to 7.6
    (c) *Both* of the above
    (d) *Neither* of the above

33. A researcher conducts a two-way analysis of variance. Factor 1 is caffeine (p. 254)
    dosage (high or low), factor 2 is gender (male or female), and the dependent
    variable is scores on a mathematics test. Which of the following indicates an
    interaction effect?
    (a) Men who receive a high dose of caffeine and women who receive a high dose of
        caffeine score higher on the test.
    * (b) Men who receive a high dose of caffeine and women who receive a low dose of
        caffeine score higher on the test.
    (c) *Both* of the above
    (d) *Neither* of the above

34. A researcher conducts a two-way analysis of variance. Factor 1 is caffeine   (p. 254)
    dosage (high or low), factor 2 is a gender (male or female), and the
    dependent variable is scores on a mathematics test. Which of the following
    indicates an *interaction* effect?
    (a) Women who receive either a high or low dose of caffeine score higher than men
        who receive either a high or low dose of caffeine.
    * (b) Men who receive a low dose of caffeine obtain higher scores than anyone else.
    (c) *Both* of the above
    (d) *Neither* of the above

Questions 35–45 refer to the data from a two-way analysis of variance shown below:

>   Total number of subjects = 36 (3 in each group)
>   Number of columns (factor 1) = 3
>   Number of rows (factor 2) = 4
>
>   Total degrees of freedom = 35
>   Degrees of freedom within groups = 24
>   Degrees of freedom between groups = 11
>
>   Total sum of squares = 40
>   Sum of squares between groups = 16
>   Sum of squares for factor 1 = 10
>   Sum of squares for factor 2 = 4

35. The within-groups sum of squares is equal to: (p. 247)
    (a) 2
    (b) 10
    * (c) 24
    (d) Cannot be determined from the information given

36. The interaction sum of squares is equal to: (p. 248)
    * (a) 2
    (b) 10
    (c) 24
    (d) Cannot be determined from the information given

37. The degrees of freedom for factor 1 is: (p. 248)
    (a) 1
    * (b) 2
    (c) 3
    (d) Cannot be determined from the information given

38. The degrees of freedom for factor 2 is: (p. 248)
    (a) 1
    (b) 2
    * (c) 3
    (d) Cannot be determined from the information given

39. The degrees of freedom for the interaction between factors 1 and 2 is: (p. 248)
    (a) 5
    * (b) 6
    (c) 7
    (d) Cannot be determined from the information given

40. The mean square for factor 1 is equal to: (p. 249)
    * (a) $10/2 = 5.0$
    (b) $10/3 = 3.33$
    (c) $10/5 = 2.0$
    (d) $10/6 = 1.67$

41. The mean square for factor 2 is equal to: (p. 249)
    (a) $4/2 = 2.0$
    * (b) $4/3 = 1.33$
    (c) $4/5 = 0.8$
    (d) $4/6 = 0.67$

42. The mean square for the interaction between factor 1 and factor 2 is equal to: (p. 249)
    (a) $24/6 = 4.0$
    (b) $2/5 = 0.4$
    (c) $10/7 = 1.43$
    * (d) $2/6 = 0.33$

43. The mean square within groups is equal to: (p. 249)
    * (a) $24/24 = 1.0$
    (b) $10/24 = 0.42$
    (c) $2/24 = 0.08$
    (d) Cannot be determined from the information given

44. The F test for the interaction is less than 1, so the interaction *cannot* be (p. 250)
    statistically significant.
    * (a) True
    (b) False

45. Which is more likely to be statistically significant, factor 1 or factor 2? (p. 250)
    * (a) Factor 1, because its F ratio is 5.0 and the F ratio for factor 2 is only 1.33
    (b) Factor 2, because its F ratio is 2.0 and the F ratio for factor 1 is only 1.67
    (c) Both factor 1 and factor 2 are equally likely to be statistically significant because their F ratios are equal.
    (d) Neither factor 1 nor factor 2 is likely to be statistically significant because both F ratios are less than 1.5.

Chapter 17

1. Which of the following should be used to test hypotheses about *frequency* data? (p. 260)
    - (a) The standard error of the mean
    - (b) The t test for the difference between two means
    - * (c) Chi square
    - (d) All of the above

2. A statistics class has 42 students. Which of the following is in the form of *frequency* data? (p. 260)
    - (a) The mean on the midterm exam is 72.4.
    - * (b) 34 students like the course and 8 students dislike it.
    - (c) *Both* of the above
    - (d) *Neither* of the above

3. A statistics class has 42 students. The instructor wishes to test the hypothesis that the number of students who like the course is equal to the number of students who dislike the course. Using chi square, what are the *expected* frequencies? (p. 261)
    - * (a) 21 and 21
    - (b) 50 and 50
    - (c) 28 and 14
    - (d) *None* of the above

4. A statistics class has 42 students. The instructor wishes to test the hypothesis that two-thirds of the students like the course. Using chi square, what are the *expected* frequencies? (p. 261)
    - (a) 21 and 21
    - (b) 28 and 0
    - * (c) 28 and 14
    - (d) *None* of the above

5. A researcher who uses chi square and wants to obtain statistically significant results would like the difference between the observed frequencies and the expected frequencies to be: (p. 261)
    - (a) small.
    - (b) medium.
    - * (c) large.
    - (d) equal to the standard deviation of the raw scores.

6. Using chi square, the sum of the expected frequencies must be equal to the sum of the observed frequencies. (p. 261)
   * (a) True
   (b) False

7. A soda manufacturer wishes to test the hypothesis that more people like his brand than Brand X. The manufacturer obtains a sample of 100 people and finds that 53 people prefer his brand and 47 prefer Brand X. In this study, chi square is equal to: (p. 261)
   (a) $9/53 + 9/47 = 0.36$
   (b) $3/50 + 3/50 = 0.12$
   * (c) $9/50 + 9/50 = 3.60$
   (d) Cannot be determined from the information given

8. A special amendment requires two-thirds of the vote to pass. For a sample of 30 voters, 22 plan to vote for the amendment and 8 plan to vote against it. In this study, chi square is equal to: (p. 261)
   (a) $49/15 + 49/15 = 6.53$
   (b) $49/22 + 49/8 = 8.35$
   (c) $4/22 + 4/8 = 0.68$
   * (d) $4/20 + 4/10 = 0.60$

9. When testing chi square for statistical significance, the degrees of freedom are equal to: (p. 262)
   (a) the number of scores.
   (b) the number of categories.
   (c) the number of scores minus one.
   * (d) the number of categories minus one.

10. A chi square of –4.27 indicates: (p. 261)
    (a) an inverse relationship between category and scores on the dependent variable.
    (b) the results are *not* statistically significant.
    (c) one or more of the assumptions underlying the use of chi square has been violated.
    * (d) an error in computation.

11. A soda manufacturer wishes to test the hypothesis that more people like her (p. 262)
    brand than Brand X. The manufacturer obtains a sample of 100 people and
    asks them whether they prefer her brand or Brand X. In this study, the chi square
    table should be entered with how many degrees of freedom?
    * (a) 1
      (b) 50
      (c) 99
      (d) 100

12. A soda manufacturer wishes to test the hypothesis that more people like her (p. 263)
    brand than Brand X. The manufacturer obtains a sample of 100 people and
    finds that 60 prefer her brand and 40 prefer Brand X. If the critical value of
    chi square needed to reject the null hypothesis is 3.84, what should the
    manufacturer decide?
      (a) More people do *not* prefer her brand.
    * (b) More than half the people in the population prefer her brand.
      (c) 60% of the people in the population prefer her brand.
      (d) *None* of the above

13. A special amendment requires two-thirds of the vote to pass. For a sample (p. 263)
    of 60 voters, 44 plan to vote for it and 16 plan to vote against it. If the critical
    value of chi square needed to reject the null hypothesis is 3.84, what decision
    should be reached?
      (a) The amendment will *not* pass.
      (b) The amendment will pass.
      (c) 73% of the population will vote for the amendment.
    * (d) *None* of the above

14. A special amendment requires two-thirds of the vote to pass. For a sample (p. 263)
    of 60 voters, 42 plan to vote for it and 18 plan to vote against it. If a chi square
    test is *not* statistically significant, the correct way to state the conclusion is:
      (a) the amendment will *not* pass.
      (b) the amendment will pass.
      (c) 70% of the population will vote for the amendment.
    * (d) there is not sufficient reason to believe that the amendment will pass.

15. A soda manufacturer wishes to test the hypothesis that more people like her (p. 263)
    brand than Brand X. The manufacturer obtains a sample of 100 people and
    finds that 70 people prefer her brand and 30 prefer Brand X. If a chi square
    test is statistically significant, the correct way to state the conclusion is:
       (a) there is not sufficient reason to believe that more people prefer her brand.
    * (b) more than half the people in the population prefer her brand.
       (c) at least 70% of the people in the population prefer her brand.
       (d) *none* of the above

16. Which of the following assumptions must be satisfied in order for chi square (p. 264)
    to give accurate results?
       (a) No response should be related to or dependent on any other response.
       (b) A subject must fall in only one category.
       (c) The computations must be based on all the subjects in the sample.
    * (d) *All* of the above
       (e) *None* of the above

17. Chi square should *not* be used if: (p. 264)
    * (a) there is one degree of freedom and one of the expected frequencies is less than 5.
       (b) there is one degree of freedom and one of the observed frequencies is less than 5.
       (c) *both* of the above
       (d) *neither* of the above

18. To test the significance of the relationship between two variables when data (p. 265)
    are in the form of frequencies, which of the following should be used?
       (a) One-way analysis of variance
       (b) Two-way analysis of variance
       (c) One-variable chi square
    * (d) Two-variable chi square

19. A researcher wishes to test the hypothesis that gender and political (p. 266)
    preference (Democrat versus Republican) are related. The researcher obtains
    a sample of 80 registered voters, and the results are: 26 men are Republicans,
    14 men are Democrats, 15 women are Republicans, and 25 women are Democrats.
    If the critical value of chi square needed to reject the null hypothesis is 3.84, what
    should the researcher decide?
       (a) Gender and political preference are *not* related.
       (b) There is not sufficient reason to believe that gender and political preference are related.
    * (c) Gender and political preference *are* related.
       (d) 65% of the men in the population are Republicans and 62.5% of the women in the population are Democrats.

20. A researcher wishes to test the hypothesis that gender and political (p. 266) preference (Democrat versus Republican) are related. The researcher obtains a sample of 80 registered voters, and the results are: 23 men are Republicans, 17 men are Democrats, 18 women are Republicans, and 22 women are Democrats. If the critical value of chi square needed to reject the null hypothesis is 3.84, what should the researcher decide?
    (a) Gender and political preference are *not* related.
    * (b) There is not sufficient reason to believe that gender and political preference are related.
    (c) Gender and political preference *are* related.
    (d) 57.5% of the men in the population are Republicans and 55% of the women in the population are Democrats.

21. A researcher wishes to test the hypothesis that men prefer Pepsi and women (p. 266) prefer Coke. The researcher obtains a sample of 80 people, and the results are as follows: 30 men prefer Coke, 10 men prefer Pepsi, 5 women prefer Coke, and 35 women prefer Pepsi. If chi square is statistically significant using the .05 criterion, what should the researcher decide?
    (a) Gender and soda preference are *not* related.
    (b) There is not sufficient reason to believe that gender and soda preference are related.
    * (c) More men prefer Coke and more women prefer Pepsi.
    (d) 75% of men in the population prefer Coke and 87.5% of the women in the population prefer Pepsi.

22. A researcher wishes to test the hypothesis that men prefer Pepsi and (p. 266) women prefer Coke. The researcher obtains a sample of 80 people, and the results are: 22 men prefer Coke, 18 men prefer Pepsi, 17 women prefer Coke, and 23 women prefer Pepsi. If chi square is *not* statistically significant using the .05 criterion, what should the researcher decide?
    (a) Gender and soda preference are *not* related.
    * (b) There is not sufficient reason to believe that gender and soda preference are related.
    (c) More men prefer Coke and more women prefer Pepsi.
    (d) 55% of the men in the population prefer Coke and 57.5% of the women in the population prefer Pepsi.

23. Which of the following is used with frequency tables that are larger (pp. 270, 272)
    than 2 × 2?
    (a) The phi coefficient
    * (b) Cramer's phi
    (c) *Both* of the above
    (d) *Neither* of the above

24. Which of the following should be converted to either a phi coefficient or (p. 270)
    Cramer's phi?
    * (a) A statistically significant chi square obtained from a two-variable analysis
    (b) A chi square from a two-variable analysis that is *not* statistically significant
    (c) *Both* of the above
    (d) *Neither* of the above

25. Which of the following should be converted to either a phi coefficient or (p. 270)
    Cramer's phi?
    (a) A statistically significant chi square obtained from a one-variable problem
    * (b) A statistically significant chi square obtained from a two-variable problem
    (c) *Both* of the above
    (d) *Neither* of the above

26. The smallest and largest values of the phi coefficient are: (p. 271)
    (a) minus infinity and plus infinity.
    (b) −4.0 and +4.0.
    * (c) −1.0 and 1.0.
    (d) 0 and plus infinity.

27. The contingency coefficient is a less desirable measure than phi or (p. 272)
    Cramer's phi because:
    (a) it can be used only with 2 × 2 tables.
    (b) it is difficult to interpret because it varies between −4.0 and +4.0.
    (c) it is more likely to cause a Type II error.
    * (d) its maximum value is affected by the size of the chi square table.

28. If a statistically significant value of chi square is converted to a phi (p. 271)
    coefficient of .12, this indicates that:
    (a) the results are likely to be useful for practical purposes.
    * (b) the results are *not* likely to be useful for practical purposes.
    (c) the experiment should be repeated with a larger sample.
    (d) an error in computation was made.

29. If a statistically significant value of chi square is converted to a phi (p. 271)
    coefficient of .57, this indicates that:
    * (a) the results are likely to be useful for practical purposes.
    (b) the results are *not* likely to be useful for practical purposes.
    (c) the experiment should be repeated with a larger sample.
    (d) an error in computation was made.

30. If a researcher converts a statistically significant chi square to a phi (p. 271)
    coefficient, the phi coefficient must be statistically significant.
    * (a) True
    (b) False

Questions 31–40 refer to the two-variable chi-square study shown below. The entries in the table represent observed frequencies.

	Men	Women
Democrats	8	2
Republicans	4	6

31. What is the *expected* frequency in the Men–Democrats cell? (p. 266)
    (a) 4
    (b) 5
    * (c) 6
    (d) Cannot be determined from the information given

32. What is the *expected* frequency in the Women–Republicans cell? (p. 266)
    * (a) 4
    (b) 5
    (c) 6
    (d) Cannot be determined from the information given

33. The sum of the *expected* frequencies for men is 12. (p. 267)
    * (a) True
    (b) False

34. The sum of the *expected* frequencies for men is equal to the sum of the (p. 267)
    expected frequencies for women.
    (a) True
    * (b) False

35. The sum of *expected* frequencies for Democrats is equal to the sum of *expected* frequencies for Republicans. (p. 267)
    * (a) True
    (b) False

36. The *expected* frequency for the Men–Democrats cell is equal to the *expected* frequency for the Women–Democrats cell. (p. 267)
    (a) True
    * (b) False

37. The *expected* frequency for the Men–Democrats cell is equal to the *expected* frequency for the Men–Republicans cell. (p. 267)
    * (a) True
    (b) False

38. The sum of all the *expected* frequencies is 20. (pp. 267–268)
    * (a) True
    (b) False

39. Chi square is equal to: (p. 261)
    (a) $9/5 + 1/5 + 9/5 + 1/5 = 4.0$
    (b) $4/4 + 4/6 + 4/4 + 0/6 = 2.67$
    (c) $16/4 + 0/4 + 16/6 + 0/6 = 5.33$
    * (d) $4/6 + 4/6 + 4/4 + 4/4 = 3.33$

40. To test this chi square for statistical significance, the chi square table should be entered with how many degrees of freedom? (p. 267)
    * (a) 1
    (b) 2
    (c) 3
    (d) 4

Chapter 18

1. A *nonparametric* statistical test: (p. 277)
    (a) does *not* use a null and alternative hypothesis.
    * (b) does *not* estimate the value of a population mean or standard deviation.
    (c) *both* of the above
    (d) *neither* of the above

2. Which of the following is a nonparametric statistical test? (p. 277)
    (a) The t test for the difference between two means
    (b) The Pearson r correlation coefficient
    (c) One-way and two-way analysis of variance
    * (d) Chi square

3. The *advantage* of using a nonparametric test is: (p. 278)
    * (a) it does not require the population being sampled to be normally distributed.
    (b) it makes a Type II error less likely.
    (c) *both* of the above
    (d) *neither* of the above

4. The *disadvantage* of using a nonparametric test is: (p. 278)
    (a) it is more likely to lead to a Type I error if the populations are normally distributed.
    * (b) it is more likely to lead to a Type II error if the populations are normally distributed.
    (c) *both* of the above
    (d) *neither* of the above

5. If a researcher uses a nonparametric test when the populations being studied are normally distributed: (p. 278)
    (a) the researcher will obtain more accurate results.
    (b) the researcher is more likely to *incorrectly* conclude that her theory has been supported.
    * (c) the researcher is more likely to *incorrectly* conclude that her theory has *not* been supported.
    (d) the .01 criterion of significance should be used instead of the .05 criterion.

6. As compared with the corresponding parametric test, a nonparametric test: (pp. 278–279)
   (a) has less power.
   (b) requires a larger sample size in order to have the same probability of rejecting a false null hypothesis.
   * (c) *both* of the above
   (d) *neither* of the above

7. To have power = .80, a parametric test requires a sample size of 70. If the *power efficiency* of the corresponding nonparametric test is 70%, what size sample does the nonparametric test require to have power = .80? (p. 279)
   (a) 49
   (b) 56
   * (c) 100
   (d) Cannot be determined from the information given

8. To have power = .75, a parametric test requires a sample size of 64. If the *power efficiency* of the corresponding nonparametric test is 80%, what size sample does the nonparametric test require to have power = .75? (p. 279)
   (a) 48
   (b) 51
   * (c) 80
   (d) Cannot be determined from the information given

9. A nonparametric test should be used when: (p. 279)
   (a) the population is normally distributed and the sample size is less than 20.
   * (b) the population distribution departs substantially from normality and the sample size is less than 20.
   (c) the population distribution departs substantially from normality and the sample size is 50 or more.
   (d) *all* of the above

10. Which of the following nonparametric tests corresponds to the t test for two independent sample means? (p. 281)
    * (a) The rank-sum test
    (b) The Kruskal-Wallis H test
    (c) The Wilcoxon test
    (d) *None* of the above

11. Which of the following nonparametric tests corresponds to the one-way (p. 287)
    analysis of variance?
    (a) The rank-sum test
    * (b) The Kruskal-Wallis H test
    (c) The Wilcoxon test
    (d) *None* of the above

12. Which of the following nonparametric tests corresponds to the matched t test? (p. 292)
    (a) The rank-sum test
    (b) The Kruskal-Wallis H test
    * (c) The Wilcoxon test
    (d) *None* of the above

13. When testing a rank sum for statistical significance, the result is referred to: (p. 283)
    * (a) the normal curve table.
    (b) the t table.
    (c) the F table.
    (d) the chi square table.

14. Compared with the corresponding parametric test, the power efficiency of (p. 284)
    the rank sum test is approximately:
    (a) 20%–25%.
    (b) 50%.
    (c) 80%–85%.
    * (d) 92%–95%.

15. If a rank sum test is statistically significant, the strength of the relationship (p. 284)
    between group membership and ranks is determined by computing:
    (a) epsilon.
    * (b) the Glass rank biserial correlation.
    (c) the matched pairs rank biserial correlation.
    (d) the phi coefficient.

16. When testing a Kruskal-Wallis H for statistical significance, the result is (p. 287)
    referred to:
    (a) the normal curve table.
    (b) the t table.
    (c) the F table.
    * (d) the chi square table.

17. Compared with the corresponding parametric test, the power efficiency of the   (p. 287)
    Kruskal-Wallis H test is approximately:
    (a) 20%–25%.
    (b) 50%.
    (c) 80%–85%.
    * (d) 90%–95%.

18. If a Kruskal-Wallis H is statistically significant, the strength of the
    relationship between group membership and ranks is determined by computing:
    * (a) epsilon.
    (b) the Glass rank biserial correlation.
    (c) the matched pairs rank biserial correlation.
    (d) the phi coefficient.

19. When performing a test of statistical significance for the Wilcoxon test, the   (p. 292)
    result is referred to:
    * (a) the normal curve table.
    (b) the t table.
    (c) the F table.
    (d) the chi square table.

20. Compared with the corresponding parametric test, the power efficiency of   (p. 292)
    the Wilcoxon test is approximately:
    (a) 20%–25%.
    (b) 50%.
    (c) 80%–85%.
    * (d) 92%–95%.

21. If the result of a Wilcoxon test is statistically significant, the strength of the   (p. 292)
    relationship between condition and the dependent variable is determined by
    computing:
    (a) epsilon.
    (b) the Glass rank biserial correlation.
    * (c) the matched pairs rank biserial correlation.
    (d) the phi coefficient.

22. For which of the following should the protected rank-sum test be used when   (p. 287)
    the overall results are statistically significant?
    (a) The rank-sum test
    * (b) The Kruskal-Wallis H test
    (c) The Wilcoxon test
    (d) *All* of the above

23. A researcher who wishes to test the difference between the locations of two (p. 281)
    independent samples by using a nonparametric test should use:
    * (a) the rank-sum test.
    (b) the Kruskal-Wallis H test.
    (c) the Wilcoxon test.
    (d) *none* of the above

24. A researcher who wishes to test the difference between the locations of two (p. 289)
    matched samples by using a nonparametric test should use:
    (a) the rank-sum test.
    (b) the Kruskal-Wallis H test.
    * (c) the Wilcoxon test.
    (d) *none* of the above

25. A researcher who wishes to test the difference between the locations of four independent
    samples by using a nonparametric test should use:
    (a) the rank-sum test.
    * (b) the Kruskal-Wallis H test.
    (c) the Wilcoxon test.
    (d) *none* of the above

26. The median test and the sign test: (p. 294)
    (a) have a power efficiency of only about 65%–70%.
    (b) should be used only as rough approximations.
    * (c) *both* of the above
    (d) *neither* of the above

27. A researcher who is using the rank-sum test and hopes to obtain statistical (p. 282)
    significance would like the difference between the sum of the ranks of Group 1
    and the expected sum of the ranks to be:
    (a) small.
    (b) medium.
    * (c) large.
    (d) equal to the standard deviation of the raw scores.

28. Using the rank-sum test, T_1 = the sum of the ranks of Group 1 and T_E = the (p. 282)
    expected sum of the ranks. If the standard error of the ranks is 15.0,
    which of the following results are statistically significant using the .05 criterion?
    (a) $T_1 = 133$, $T_E = 115$
    * (b) $T_1 = 101$, $T_E = 138$
    (c) *Both* of the above
    (d) *Neither* of the above

29. Using the rank-sum test, T_1 = the sum of the ranks of Group 1. If the expected sum of the ranks is 115 and the standard error of the ranks is 15.0, which of the following values of T_1 will produce statistically significant results using the .05 criterion?   (p. 282)
    (a) 159
    (b) 145
    * (c) *Both* of the above
    (d) *Neither* of the above

30. The Glass rank biserial correlation coefficient: (p. 284)
    (a) is the same as a Pearson r computed on the ranks.
    * (b) may take on values from –1.0 to +1.0.
    (c) *both* of the above
    (d) *neither* of the above

31. A researcher who is using the Kruskal-Wallis H test hopes to obtain statistical significance. The researcher would like the sums of the ranks of the groups in the study to be: (p. 286)
    (a) equal to each other.
    * (b) very different from each other.
    (c) close to the expected sums of the ranks.
    (d) equal to N (N + 1) / 2.

32. A Kruskal-Wallis H test includes four groups and nine subjects. If SS_B = 30 and H = $12 SS_B$ / N (N + 1), H is equal to: (p. 287)
    * (a) (12) (30) / (9) (10) = 4.0
    (b) (12) (30) / (4) (5) = 18.0
    (c) (12) (30) / (13) (14) = 1.98
    (d) *None* of the above

33. A researcher who is using the Wilcoxon test hopes to obtain statistical significance. The researcher would prefer which of the following sets of difference scores?   (p. 290)
    (a) –8, –7, –4, –2, +2, +5, +6, +50
    (b) –2, –2, –1, 0, +1, +1, +2, +2
    * (c) –9, –7, –6, –5, +1, +1, +2, +2, +3, +3, +3
    (d) –15, –12, –10, –10, +10, +11, +11, +15

34. Using the Wilcoxon test, T_1 = the sum of the ranks of Group 1 and T_E = the expected sum of the ranks. If the standard error of the ranks is 9.0, which of the following results is statistically significant using the .05 criterion? (p. 291)
   * (a) T_1 = 53.5, T_E = 33
   (b) T_1 = 23, T_E = 33
   (c) *Both* of the above
   (d) *Neither* of the above

35. Using the Wilcoxon test, T_1 = the sum of the ranks of Group 1. If the expected sum of the ranks is 33 and the standard error of the ranks is 11.0, which of the following values of T_1 will produce statistically significant results using the .05 criterion? (p. 291)
   (a) 10
   (b) 60
   * (c) *Both* of the above
   (d) *Neither* of the above

36. Statistically significant results are obtained for a Kruskal-Wallis H test with four groups. To perform a protected rank-sum test for Groups 1 and 2, the scores in these two groups must be reranked by ignoring Groups 3 and 4. (p. 288)
   * (a) True
   (b) False

37. The matched-pairs rank biserial correlation: (p. 293)
   (a) is the same as a Pearson r computed on the ranks.
   * (b) may take on values from –10 to +1.0.
   (c) *both* of the above
   (d) *neither* of the above

38. The sum of the ranks from 1 to N is equal to: (p. 280)
   (a) 2N + N / 2
   (b) N (N – 1) / 2
   * (c) N (N + 1) / 2
   (d) *None* of the above

39. When testing the results of a median test for statistical significance, the results are referred to: (p. 295)
   (a) the normal curve table.
   (b) the t table.
   (c) the F table.
   * (d) the chi square table.

40. When testing the results of a sign test for statistical significance, the results (p. 298)
    are referred to:
    (a) the normal curve table.
    (b) the t table.
    (c) the F table.
    * (d) the chi square table.